Do we really need another book on the apologetics of C.S. Lewis, since there are so many other able treatments available? If it is this book, then, yes, there is such a need. Donald Williams makes a unique, helpful, and skillful contribution to the literature on Lewis in particular and apologetics in general. I plan to use *Answers from Aslan* as a textbook the next time I teach The Apologetics of C.S. Lewis, and I heartily endorse it for anyone interested in this subject. May it advance the rational case for Christianity in our day.

Douglas Groothuis
Professor of Philosophy, Denver Seminary
Author of *Christian Apologetics: A Comprehensive Case for Biblical Faith*

What a splendid, elegant, and practical book *Answers from Aslan* is! On the writing of books on C.S. Lewis there seems to be no end, yet this book makes a unique and valuable contribution not only to the field of Lewis studies but also to the field of Christian apologetics. Donald Williams is unquestionably a master guide through Lewis's major apologetic works (he is one of my go-to scholars on Lewis), Williams is also one of the wisest and most skilled apologists writing today. *Answers from Aslan* is not only a book that should be read by all apologists—it's a book that should be read by all of us, myself included. I cannot recommend this book to you more highly. Buy it, read it, re-read it, and implement its lessons. You won't be disappointed.

Robert B. Stewart
Professor of Philosophy and Theology
New Orleans Baptist Theological Seminary

Donald Williams is a man whom God has equipped to serve "such a time as this." Yet, truth is timeless and able to be applied to yesterday, today, and tomorrow. Knowing how to relate truth and read the times is wisdom and ought to be considered a gift from God. God is the source and grantor of all such wisdom. C.S. Lewis was just such a man whom God equipped with wisdom to reach the world for the cause of Christ.

Donald Williams embodies Lewis's legacy, both as a man God has equipped with biblical wisdom and the power of the pen to communicate to this post-Christian world. Through this book, Williams equips a new generation to learn from the best Lewis has to offer and apply it to the present-day. *Tolle lege.*

William C. Roach
Dean of the Normal L. Geisler Chair of Christian Apologetics
Veritas International University

Don Williams, a world-class apologist in his own right, is one of America's leading C.S. Lewis scholars. Don is able to grasp the apologetic insights of C.S. Lewis, regardless of whether he is dealing with Lewis's non-fiction or fiction. He is able to break down and explain the profound insights of C.S. Lewis for a new generation. He shows how the apologetic thought of C.S. Lewis is still relevant to our culture—even though our culture has gone through radical transformation. Christian apologists should be thankful not only for the work and thought of C.S. Lewis, but also for the brilliance of Professor Don Williams for interpreting and articulating the ideas of Lewis for contemporary man. I highly recommend this work, and any other of Don's books dealing with the apologetic work of C.S. Lewis.

Phil Fernandes
President of the International Society of Christian Apologetics
Pastor, Trinity Bible Fellowship
Adjunct Professor, Veritas International University;
Northwest University

If you were in search of a book written by an apologist, a philosopher, a theologian, a pastor, and a poet, what might a book like that look like? It would look a lot like this one by Donald Williams. Don clearly points out that the Lord redeems the whole person, not just the soul, the heart, the mind, or the body, but the whole person. He takes to heart the Greatest Commandment (Matt 22.37) in a way that few seem to understand or practice. It is also clear that the Great Commission was to make disciples, not just converted souls. This is woven through the entirety of the book. Apologetics is a tool for the defense of the gospel, preparing the way for the presentation of the gospel and discipling those who have embraced the gospel with the intent of pointing to the One whose death, burial, and physical resurrection are the gospel. Those who read this volume will be challenged, comforted, and from time discover themselves worshipping the One that is the author and finisher of our faith!

L.L. (Don) Veinot, Jr.
President, Midwest Christian Outreach, Inc.

Some may argue Lewis's apologetic approaches are outdated. Williams clearly does not hold this perspective that smacks of chronological snobbery. However, in *Answers from Aslan*, Williams is well aware that because of shifts in culture, there is a need to make some adjustments to apply the seven different approaches Lewis uses in defending the faith. After providing five theses on why apologetics is even needed, Williams provides excellent summaries of each approach, gives an honest critique of them, and then shares useful ways to apply them in today's world.

William O'Flaherty
Creator of *Knowing and Understanding C.S. Lewis* YouTube Channel
Author of *The Misquotable C.S. Lewis*

Donald Williams's *Answers from Aslan* offers a detailed, helpful survey and evaluation of the various apologetic arguments of C.S.

Lewis. Williams avoids the pitfall of treating imagination and intellect as being in tension, just as Lewis himself avoided it, and this understanding allows him to explain precisely how storytelling fits into a robustly evidence-based Christianity. The inclusion of Williams's own poems as interludes between chapters fits with this overarching theme of a union between the aesthetic and analytical aspects of the Christian mind.

Lydia McGrew
Author of *Testimonies to the Truth: Why You Can Trust the Gospels*

ANSWERS FROM ASLAN

Answers From Aslan

The Enduring Apologetics of C.S. Lewis

Donald T. Williams

DeWard
for your journey

Answers from Aslan: The Enduring Apologetics of C.S. Lewis
© 2023 by DeWard Publishing Company, Ltd.
P.O. Box 290696, Tampa, FL 33687
www.deward.com

Cover by Barry Wallace.

Printed in the United States of America.

ISBN: 978-1-947929-28-9

*To the students across the years in my C. S. Lewis seminar
and my Apologetics course at Toccoa Falls College
and at Summit Semester.*

Further up and further in!

CONTENTS

ACKNOWLEDGEMENTS

A number of these chapters had previous lives as journal articles and other publications. Earlier versions of the Introduction appeared as "The Complete Apologist: Four Essentials Every Christian is Called to Embrace," *Touchstone: A Journal of Mere Christianity*, 34:4 (July-August 2021): 38–42 and as a chapter, "Five theses on Apologetics" in *Ninety-Five Theses for a New Reformation: A Road Map for Post-Evangelical Christianity* (Toccoa: *Semper Reformanda* Publications, 2021): 244–61. An earlier version of chapter 2 appeared as "Anselm and Aslan: C.S. Lewis and the Ontological Argument." *Touchstone: A Journal of Mere Christianity* 27:6 (Nov.-Dec., 2014): 36–39. An earlier version of chapter 3 appeared as "Printing Error: On Anscombe's Final Word on Lewis and Naturalism," *Touchstone: A Journal of Mere Christianity* 29:3 (May-June 2016): 20–22. Chapter 4 started life as "Lacking, Ludicrous, or Logical? The Validity of Lewis's 'Trilemma,'" *Midwestern Journal of Theology* 11:1 (Spring 2012): 91–102. It was then expanded as "Pro: A Defense of C.S. Lewis's 'Trilemma'" for *C.S. Lewis's Apologetics: Pro and Con*, ed. Gregory Bassham (Leiden: Brill/Rodopi, 2015): 171–89 and reprinted by permission as "Excursus on the Trilemma" in *Deeper Magic: The Theology behind the Writings of C.S. Lewis* (Baltimore, Md: Square Halo Books, 2016): 129–47. An earlier version of chapter 5 appeared as "Made for Another World: C.S. Lewis's Argument from Desire Revisited" *Philosophia Christi: The Journal of the Evangelical Philosophical Society* 19:2 (2018): 449–54. An earlier version of chapter 8 appeared as "Answers for Orual: C.S. Lewis as a role Model for Winsome Apologists," (2016 Presidential Address from the annual meeting of the International Society for Christian Apologetics), *The Journal of the International Society of Christian Apologetics* 10:1 (March, 2017): 5–20. An earlier version of chapter 8 was "Meaningful Truth: The Critical Role of Imagination in the Work of C.S. Lewis," *Touchstone: A Journal of Mere Christianity* 31:6 (Nov.-Dec., 2018): 34–37.

The poems that appear here as interludes are from *Stars through the Clouds: The Collected Poetry of Donald T. Williams*, 2nd ed. (Lynchburg, Va: Lantern Hollow Press, 2020) or are previously unpublished.

All these works appear here by permission.

C.S. Lewis introduced me to apologetics when I started reading him in the early seventies, and he helped preserve my own faith, which was under assault from the anti-intellectualism in the church. Mentors who confirmed my love for Lewis as a door to truth and got me off on the right foot as a student of him included Frances White Ewbank, my undergraduate adviser at Taylor University, and Clyde S. Kilby, who directed the "Junior Practicum" I spent at the Lewis collection at Wheaton College. I was fortunate to study apologetics under John Warwick Montgomery at Trinity Evangelical Divinity School. My fellow Lewis scholars and fellow apologists and the three decades of students who were members of Inklings II, the Christian writers group I led at Toccoa Falls College, or who took my C.S. Lewis and Apologetics courses there, are too numerous to mention. But sharing their love of Lewis and of Christian truth over the years has helped to make this book possible. Any errors or imperfections of fact, thought, or style that have crept their way into it are definitely my own.

Lewis was not perfect, but he was a signpost in the wilderness pointing me to Jerusalem. If this book helps him continue to be that for you and for the next generation, it will achieve its purpose.

FOREWORD

Like many Christian apologists, I savor and often return to the work of C.S. Lewis in defending the Christian faith as true, rational, and pertinent to life. My reading of *Mere Christianity*, *Miracles*, and *The Abolition of Man* in college forged and formed me as a Christian thinker who became unafraid to critically challenge other worldviews and who was willing to defend my own rationally. I often quote him in my writing[1] and have taught a course at Denver Seminary on his apologetics for over twenty-five years. The material never gets old, and my students always benefit.

But do we really need another book on the apologetics of C.S. Lewis, since there are so many other able treatments available? If it is this book, then there is such a need, because Professor Donald Williams makes a unique, helpful, and skillful contribution to the literature on Lewis in particular and apologetics in general.

Unlike many writers, C.S. Lewis is a deep well of reason, imagination, and wisdom pertaining to the Christian faith—to apologetics and to the spiritual life in general. As such, he offers a rich resource for discussion, analysis, and critique decade-after-decade. Despite the vast secondary literature that Lewis has generated, all that is important about his thinking has not yet been written. There is more to draw out of his well. Further, Lewis's apologetics,

---

[1] A general search of the Kindle version of my book, *Christian Apologetics: A Comprehensive Case for Biblical Faith*, 2nd ed. (Downers Grove, IL: InterVarsity Press, 2022) yields ninety-six references, including footnotes.

while fundamentally solid and profound, needs to be brought into contemporary discussions about the issues he raises.

Professor Williams combines the virtues needed to produce another book on Lewis's apologetics. First, he writes lucidly about challenging topics and the chapters are well-organized, with an emphasis on *actually using Lewis's apologetics today*. Second, he is well-versed in both Lewis's corpus and the pertinent secondary sources (positive and negative) about Lewis's defense of Christianity. Moreover, he is equally skilled in handling both Lewis's fiction and nonfiction writings as they pertain to apologetics. Fourth, he carefully assesses the strengths and limitations of Lewis's arguments, and augments these arguments with his own contributions. This is especially evident in his chapters on the Argument from Reason and the Trilemma. Fifthly, the reader is treated to a number of fine poems written by Professor Williams, all of which perfectly complement the prose of the rest of the book.

I am planning on using *Answers from Aslan* as a textbook the next time I teach The Apologetics of C.S. Lewis, and I heartily endorse it for anyone interested in this subject. May it advance the rational case for Christianity in our day.

Douglas Groothuis
Professor of Philosophy
Denver Seminary

PRELUDE

COMMENTARY, 1 PETER 3.15

We are to keep ourselves in readiness
    Should any ask a reason for the hope
    That is within us and which we confess.
The great Deceiver does not sleep or rest,
    Enticing people toward the slippery slope,
    And so we keep ourselves in readiness.
The Truth is lovely in a silken dress;
    Her servant comes in sackcloth tied with rope,
    A humble penitent who must confess
His great unworthiness, but also stress
    Her grace, the only reason he can cope,
    And thus he keeps himself in readiness.
We are but beggars sharing our success
    With other tramps who also want to grope
    Toward the light with us. And we confess
That ours is not the brilliance we express.
    Christ is the Light; we aim the telescope:
    That's how we keep ourselves in readiness
To justify the great Hope we confess.

INTRODUCTION

The Spiritually Prepared Apologist
Five Theses on Apologetics

This is a book on C. S. Lewis as a role model for Christian apologists. It deals with the validity of his arguments to the end of asking how they might best be adjusted or nuanced to be employed most effectively in today's apologetic environment—for the world is a very different place than it was eighty years ago when Lewis was writing. (Yes, for a lot of his books it has really been that long!) But before we turn to Lewis's contributions to apologetics, we need first to think about apologetics itself. For conservative Christians are by no means unified on the questions of what apologetics is, what is its proper place in our theology, our evangelism, and the Christian life (if it has one at all), and how it should be pursued. We will best receive Lewis's help in these matters if we can get some clarity about them before we ask him for it. That is what this introduction will try to achieve.

If we treat our own faith as if it were indefensible, how must the world perceive it?

American conservative Christians are not as biblical as they think they are. In support of this claim we need look no further than the fact that, while we are clearly commanded always to be ready to make a defense to anyone who asks a reason for the hope that is within us (1 Pet 3.15), vast swaths of our adherents think it is somehow unspiritual to obey this biblical commandment. Things are better than they were a couple of generations ago. We now have a veritable Apologetics Industrial Complex and a horde of consumers interested enough to keep it in business. (Full disclosure: I must confess to being a part of it.) But it has virtually no influence on the rank and file in the pews or on the conduct of daily life in the church or on the practice of evangelism outside the relatively closed circle of apologetics nerds.[2] Why? One reason may be that we have given inadequate attention to apologetics as a *ministry* requiring a very particular type of *spiritual*—not just intellectual—preparation. I will try to make a start toward filling that gap with five theses.

---

[2] Further reading on apologetics: For a brilliant analysis of the apologetic situation that is still prophetically relevant, Francis Schaeffer, *The God Who is There: Speaking Historic Christianity into the Twentieth Century* (Downers Grove, Il.: InterVarsity, 1968); for an excellent comprehensive textbook, Douglas Groothuis, *Christian Apologetics: A Comprehensive Case for Biblical Faith* (Downers Grove, Il.: InterVarsity, 2022). Classic works by C. S. Lewis include *Mere Christianity* (NY: MacMillan, 1943), for The Moral Argument for Theism, The Trilemma, and The Argument from Desire; *Miracles: A Preliminary Study* (NY: MacMillan, 1947) for supernaturalism and the Argument from Reason; and *The Problem of Pain* (NY: MacMillan, 1967) on theodicy. For a classic work on the historical argument for the resurrection of Christ, see Frank Morison, *Who Moved the Stone?* (Downers Grove, Il.: InterVarsity, n.d.). A good short work on the trustworthiness of Scripture is F. F. Bruce, *The New Testament Documents: Are They Reliable?* (Downers Grove, Il.: InterVarsity, 1960). For general works see also William Lane Craig, *Reasonable Faith: Christian Truth and Apologetics* (Wheaton: Crossway, 1984), J. P. Moreland, *Scaling the Secular City: A Defense of Christianity* (Wheaton: Baker, 1987), and Donald T. Williams, *Reflections from Plato's Cave: Essays in Evangelical Philosophy* (Lynchburg, Va: Lantern Hollow Press, 2012) and *The Young Christian's Survival Guide: Common Questions Young Christians are Asked about God, the Bible, and the Christian Faith Answered* (Cambridge, OH: Christian Publishing House, 2019). A useful reference work is the *New Dictionary of Christian Apologetics*, ed. W. C. Campbell-Jack and Gavin McGrath (Downers Grove, Il.: InterVarsity, 2006). For advanced students, Stuart C. Hackett, *The Resurrection of Theism: Prolegomena to Christian Apology* (Grand Rapids, Mi: Baker, 1957).

Thesis 1: We are commanded to be always ready to give a defense (Greek: ἀπολογία, *apologia*) to anyone who asks a reason for the hope that is within us (1 Pet 3.15).

1 Peter 3.15 is often cited as a prooftext in favor of Christian apologetics—rightly so. Often the context is not noted, but it adds a pertinent level of understanding to what is being asked of us. The commandment is part of an ongoing discussion of persecution from chapter 2 that resumes in verse 8. In such times, Christians are to return good for evil and blessing for curses (3.8). They are to be zealous for good, make sure that if they suffer it is for righteousness, and not be intimidated or troubled (3.13–14). Instead of all that, they are commanded to "sanctify Christ as Lord in your hearts, always being ready to make a defense to anyone who asks you to give an account for the hope that is in you, yet with gentleness and reverence" (3.15). Then the discussion continues, circling back to the topic of persecution. The result of this defense is that those who slander Christians will be put to shame by the Christians' good behavior in Christ (3.16).

The context does not lessen the emphasis on rational apologetics but roots it in the realities of life. That is why the actual imperative verb, the command, of verse 15, is to "*sanctify* Christ as Lord in your hearts." We are to set Christ apart as absolute monarch of our central, inner personality, in other words. In biblical terms, He is to be Lord of the central core of our personality, the unity from which flows the distinct faculties of our intellect, our will, and our emotions. (In biblical usage, the heart is not a symbol for the feelings, as it is in modern English, but rather for that central core of the whole personality.) Then, when people see how we respond to persecution, returning good for evil and blessing for curses, they will be astonished, and they will want to know how and why we do such a thing. (Maybe if we had truly sanctified Christ as Lord on such a deep level, we would get more people asking such questions!) When they do, we need to be prepared with a reasoned response, a defense delivered not as a counterattack but rather with gentleness and reverence. So that's what apologetics is supposed to look like! Maybe there would be less resistance to it among believers themselves if it more often did.

The "account" (NASB) or in some translations "defense" we are to be ready for is the Greek word *apologia*, from which we get the English word *apologetics*. It was a legal term that referred to the final summation a lawyer would make to the judge or the jury in defense of his client. In it he would be expected to present the evidence for his client's innocence along with sound reasoning about that evidence to lead the jury to the correct verdict: acquittal. There is then good and sufficient evidence for why our hope is not misplaced, and there are rational reasons for why Christians hold to it that we need to know and be prepared to present. This readiness, this preparedness, is commanded. It is not optional. It is an integral part of making Christ Lord of your heart. It is therefore for every believer, not just for nerds and intellectuals. What we often miss is that it is part of a *spiritual* readiness that flows from Christ's lordship over our total personality. When it is abstracted from that context, or even not sufficiently rooted in it, it often does more harm than good.

No option is permitted. The commandment includes both message and manner, both substance and style. It is a rational defense requiring preparation (message, substance) which is delivered with gentleness and reverence (manner, style). And that gentleness and reverence, to be genuine, can only flow from the sanctifying of Christ in the heart which is the only root from which a healthy apologetic can grow. We are not obeying the commandment if we have mastered every argument and can run posers on intellectual websites or even real scholars who are skeptics through with the rapier of our intellect. Nor are we fulfilling its requirements if we are wonderfully nice people whose courage and hope in the midst of suffering or even persecution makes our neighbors scratch their heads, but then we have nothing to tell them but "just believe." No. What is demanded is the same kind of wholeness that Paul expressed in the phrase "speaking the truth in love" (Eph 4.15): not either/or, but both/and. Most of us, including some who actually believe in and think we are practicing biblical apologetics, are simply in disobedience here. And the Reformation the church needs in this area, if it is to begin with us at all, must begin with obedience.

Thesis 2: Apologetics is therefore an essential part of christian discipleship.

If a disciple is a person seeking to be obedient to all of Jesus' commands (according to the Great Commission), and if Jesus gave us this one through His Apostle Peter, then a disciple must be a person who aspires to obey the command to be always ready to make a defense, *and* aspires to be the kind of person whose response to suffering and persecution, flowing from the Lordship of Christ over his whole heart, invites the questions that this defense is designed to answer. Apologetics thus understood is therefore an essential part of Christian discipleship. The mere existence of the biblical commandment is sufficient in itself to make this point, but there is more to be said about why the Lord considers it a commandment important enough to have been given in the New Testament to His church. Christian apologetics is based on a biblical precept, a biblical precedent, and a biblical principle.

The biblical precept is the command of 1 Peter 3.15 that we have just been expounding. It should be seen not as an isolated injunction but as a special application of the Great Commission (Matt 28.18–20). It is also a special application of the mandated teaching ministry of the church, which has the goal of "equipping the saints for the work of service" (Eph 4.12) by grounding them in the divine Word that is profitable for teaching "so that the man of God may be adequate, equipped for every good work" (2 Tim 3.17). In that teaching ministry, "We proclaim Him [Christ], admonishing every man and teaching every man with all wisdom so that we may present every man complete in Christ" (Col 1.28). The completeness referred to in several of these passages surely includes the preparation called for by Peter's apologetic command. Apologetics is then relevant not only to evangelistic preaching but also to the proclamation of the Word that edifies and equips the saints for ministry that takes place both within and outside of the walls of the church. In all of this we respond also to Jude's appeal that we "contend earnestly for the faith that was once delivered to the saints" (Jude 1.3).

The biblical precedent is the example set by the Apostles, particularly Paul in the book of Acts, of integrating apologetics seamlessly into their proclamation. Luke sets the stage for the Apostles' preaching by noting that Jesus had presented Himself to the disciples by "many convincing proofs" (Acts 1.3). Then the early Christians preach as if they had that kind of foundation to build their message on. It is instructive to note how frequently verbs like "reasoned," "argued," and "persuaded" or conjunctive adverbs like "therefore" appear in the narrative. Peter's Pentecost sermon sets the precedent: It appeals to both the disciples' experience and to the Old Testament, concluding with a rousing "*Therefore* let all the house of Israel know for certain that God has made Him both Lord and Christ—this Jesus whom you crucified" (Acts 2.36, emphasis added). They could know of the Messiahship of Jesus with confidence because of the logical connections of the conclusion to the evidence that had been so clearly and powerfully presented.

The Apostle Paul is the Apostle of grace *par excellence*, and he is the Apostle of apologetics *par excellence* too. He began his public ministry after his conversion by "*proving*" to the Jews in Damascus that Jesus was the Christ (Acts 9.22). He did this by "*arguing*" (9.29). In Thessalonica he "*reasoned*" and "*gave evidence*" (17.2–3). Luke calls the Bereans "noble" because they thought Paul's claims through for themselves, "examining the Scriptures daily to see whether these things be so" (Acts 17.11). Paul is next found "*reasoning*" with the Greeks in Athens (Acts 17.17). At the end of his Areopagus sermon, he claims that the historical resurrection is "*proof*" that God was revealed in Christ (Acts 17.31). The Athenian philosophers were a tough audience (in a different way than the Jews had been), but some, including Dionysius and Damaris, were saved.

There are those who criticize Paul for his apologetic approach in Athens, blaming it for his limited success there and claiming that he then returned to just preaching the Word, the "simple Gospel." I think most of us would give our right arm for the assurance that we would have a few converts from even our most skeptical audiences! But the real response to that view is simply to point out that Paul's practice was consistent. He did not start reasoning and persuading in Athens; he had been doing it all along, and he kept right on doing it after he left. We next find him in Corinth, *"reasoning* in the synagogue every Sabbath and trying to *persuade* Jews and Greeks"(Acts 18.4). And it's not just Paul. After his further instruction by Priscilla and Aquila, Apollos is described as a big help because he "powerfully *refuted* the Jews in public, *demonstrating* by the Scriptures that Jesus was the Christ" (Acts 18.28, emphasis added). Then we move on to Ephesus and the focus switches back to Paul, *"reasoning* and *persuading"* (Acts 19.8). Back in Jerusalem, he gives an *apologia* before the Jews who had rioted in the Temple (Acts 22.1)—the same word used by Peter in 1 Peter 3.15. He uses the verb form of that word to describe his defense to Felix (Acts 24.10). He spends his time under house arrest in Rome at the end of the book "trying to *persuade"* the Jews about Jesus (Acts 28.23). And some of them were persuaded (Acts 28.24).

There is a consistent pattern in Paul's arguments. He appeals to premises which he can expect his audience to accept as real evidence and tries to persuade them that this evidence supports the claims of Jesus to be Lord and Christ. With Jewish audiences he appeals to the Old Testament, because they were supposed already to accept it as the Word of God. With Greeks he might appeal to general revelation, the witness of Nature to her Creator. With everyone he appeals to the historical resurrection which "was not done in a corner" (Acts 26.26). There were five hundred eyewitnesses to it, most of whom are still alive (1 Cor 15.6). Finally, he adds his own eyewitness testimony, granted on the Road to Damascus (1 Cor 15.8). The biblical precedent is clear: Peter was not asking us to do anything that the Apostles had not already practiced, setting us an example of faithful witness.

The biblical principle is that God wants to save whole people, their minds as well as their emotions, their intellects as well as their wills. Jesus went out of His way to establish this principle in His explanation of the Greatest Commandment: to "love the Lord your God with all your heart, and with all your soul, *and with all your mind*" (Matt 22.37, emphasis added). Surely when we preach the Gospel, we are calling people to love God that way in the light of His glorious grace shown to us in Christ. Therefore, the Gospel should be addressed to the whole person, including the mind. It does not mean we should speak only to intellectuals, or in a way that only intellectuals will be able to understand. It does mean that we present the Gospel as if we actually thought it was true, as something that can be thought about as well as felt, as something that can stand up to the rough and tumble of rational investigation, and as something that will affect the whole life of the person we are trying to reach.

There is then not only a biblical precept but also a precedent and a principle in favor of the proposition that apologetics—being always prepared to give a rational defense of the hope that is within us—is an essential part of Christian discipleship. Not everyone is called to major in apologetic ministry of course, but everyone is called to sanctify Christ as Lord in their hearts and to realize that this includes treating the Gospel as something that is actually true in the real world. We are given a command, good examples of people following that command, and a principle that explains why it is important to do so. And the principle is so basic, yet so little understood, that it deserves a thesis of its own.

Thesis 3: God purposes to save whole persons, which includes their minds as well as their hearts.

In a number of these theses we keep coming back to the fact that much of contemporary American Christianity has in many ways absorbed the fragmented view of life that is typical of the modern world. Why? Because we have not truly sanctified Christ as Lord in our hearts. If we had, we would realize that God made people to be, and means people to be, whole persons. We have bodies as well as souls, minds as well as hearts. The ministry of the church should therefore rebuild those whole persons out of the fragments created by sin. It is not to reinforce that fragmentation by valuing souls over bodies while aiming only at hearts and disparaging minds. The impact of this fragmented view of human nature makes itself felt in many ways. We refer to effective evangelists as "soul winners" and think of their purpose as "saving souls"—as if God were not interested in saving *people*—whole people, including both soul and body.

Growing up "In *all* aspects... into *Christ*" can mean nothing less than that the Church is trying to grow people who think like the One who designed the stars, who astounded the rabbis, and who defeated the Pharisees. It is trying to grow people who imagine the world like the One who spoke the parables. It is trying to grow people who make choices like the One whose meat and drink was to do the will of his Father. It is trying to grow people who serve like the One who washed his disciples' feet. And it is trying to grow people who love like the One who died on Calvary. It is trying to grow people who see all these acts as essential parts of an indissoluble unity whose Center is the very character of its Lord. Getting saved, accepting Christ as one's Savior and Lord, means setting out on that road. What else could it mean?

If one reform we need is to start thinking of the Christian life and of church ministry in such terms, and if evangelism means inviting people to become disciples of Jesus in such terms, to the end that they might become whole persons, then surely the Gospel should be presented as something relevant to the enquiring mind as well as the searching "heart" (modern meaning). We start where people are. We do not foolishly burden seekers with a curriculum of answers to questions they are not asking as a set of hurdles they must clear before coming to faith. But at the same time, we are presenting a message that consists of truth claims—claims that need to be pressed as such. Such claims have the inherent potential to raise apologetic questions, and we are required to be ready to deal with them when they do. Besides, if we are not presenting the Gospel as *truth*, we are not presenting the biblical Gospel at all. The enquiring mind may not be engaged at first in every case, but the very nature of the Gospel is that it will tend to engage it. We are after all asking for allegiance to a Lord who is the Way and the Truth as well as the Life.

We need to present the Gospel as a message that is addressed to the whole person, is relevant to the whole person, promises to transform the whole person, and therefore asks for a response from the whole person—including the mind. This is what the biblical writers mean when they tell us that the Gospel is addressed to the heart and needs to be believed in the heart (Rom 10.9–10). Therefore, apologetics might not be the central thrust of our dealing with any given person, but it is always lurking just beneath the surface. When the truth question comes up, we need to be prepared to deal with it honestly and with confidence. When it does not come up in a "post-truth world," we may need to bring it up ourselves. Otherwise, we are being less than honest about what we are asking people to commit to. Whether we are confronted by believers wrestling with doubts or enquirers raising objections, if we say, or even imply, "Don't ask questions—just believe," we are simply being disobedient to the command of our Lord through His Apostle. To repent of that disobedience is a reform that has been a long time coming to much of American conservative Christianity.

Thesis 4: Apologetics seeks to win people, not arguments; nevertheless, sound arguments should be employed because not to do so is to insult and blaspheme the God of truth.

Apologetics is a necessary aspect of holistic discipleship; it is also a dangerous one; and this is one reason why the spiritual preparation I have been stressing is so desperately needed. I say this as a practitioner who is fully aware that I am highly susceptible to its pitfalls and have to guard against them vigilantly. Apologetics is especially dangerous to those who are naturally prone to pursue it. We have egos. We like winning arguments. In fact, we relish demolishing our opponents, crushing them into dust, and receiving the accolades and ovations of those who already agree with us as we do so. Oh, wait. That does not actually sound much like the kind of apologetic that the context of Peter's command seems to call for. It doesn't sound much like the way people doing it for the spiritual reasons Peter gives us would operate. Oops.

The goal of Christian apologetics of course is not to win arguments; it is to win people. It is to win people to Christ, to remove obstacles to their belief in Him, and to help the faith they will come to have in Him be one that has integrity and flows from their whole personality, not just from an emotional response.

What does this look like when we are doing it as part of sanctifying Christ as Lord in our hearts? We want to remove obstacles to their belief in Him because they are obstacles to seeing Him as He is *and loving Him*. We want their faith in Him to be more than an emotional response because we understand that love is more than an emotional response, and we want them to love Him deeply, like we do, with all their souls and all their might and all their minds. They will find it hard to love Jesus that way unless they see something in us as His representatives that does not completely repel them. And guess what? The experience of being defeated and then subjected to a victory dance performed over your supine carcass is not exactly conducive to seeing your conversation partner that way.

The difficulty is, of course, that we cannot make the case for the truth of our claims about Christ without winning arguments. You have to show that your view is based on a better sampling of real evidence and the other view (the one your potential convert probably picked up from his secular society) is not. You have to show that your view is a logical conclusion reached by valid argument from that evidence, and the other one is not. Your potential disciple has picked up, and may strongly adhere to and zealously defend, ideas that come straight from the Enemy himself. It is easy to forget that this potential disciple is not the Enemy, but rather one his victims. If he is not someone you are trying to reach but rather someone attacking you as if you were both a superstitious misleader of the masses and an idiot (and you are going to attract that kind of attention if your apologetic becomes known), that mistake is especially easy to make. I used to make it all the time, and I am still trying to wean myself from it completely. It is never helpful. So we have to win arguments *in such a way* that we can also win people.

It is the old difficulty of speaking the truth in love. I can speak the truth. (I think I'm actually somewhat good at that.) I can be nice to people I disagree with. (That comes a little less naturally, but I can do it.) Doing both at the same time? That takes dependence on the Holy Spirit. And that takes a kind of death to self (another biblical way of saying "sanctify Christ as Lord in your heart") that does not come naturally at all. It is why it is absolutely necessary that apologetics begin where Peter said it should begin: with "Sanctify Christ as Lord in your hearts."

We have to win arguments in such a way that we can also win people. Addiction to winning arguments at all costs is an insidious malady to overcome. It is like food addiction. If you are addicted to alcohol or drugs or gambling and get to the point where you are finally serious about getting your life back, you can go cold turkey and give those things up completely. You learn to live without them. It is (relatively) clean and uncomplicated: You walk away and never look back. It isn't easy, but you have to do it. But if you are addicted to comfort food, you have an even more difficult struggle. You cannot just walk away from food and never look back, or you won't be living very long at all. You have to look back all the time. That is the position we are in with winning arguments instead of people. If you give up arguments altogether, you are no longer doing biblical apologetics. We have no choice but to do the dying to self which alone can make it possible for the Holy Spirit to use us.

If we must use arguments, they had better be good ones. The need to present them in love does not absolve us from the responsibility to make them evidentially rich and logically rigorous. This will be a place, as we shall see, where C. S. Lewis can greatly help us. "'Logic!' said the Professor half to himself. 'Why don't they teach logic at these schools?'"³ Well, they should. And if the public schools won't, Sunday Schools should. There's a radical reform we could implement in the church!

We serve a God who is the God of truth and whose Son is the Way, the Truth, and the Life (John 14.6). We cannot serve Him with lies. We serve a God whose character is the ground of logic. It is because He cannot lie (Titus 1.2) that the law of non-contradiction is universally valid in every possible world.⁴ We cannot serve Him with fallacies. To try to do so is to blaspheme His name, because it implies that He is not true. Any such apologetic would undercut itself at every turn. In every area of endeavor, we should give Him the best of which we are capable, not because it is adequate but because He deserves nothing less. This is especially true in apologetics, where we are directly representing Him as Truth and as true: The truth of His existence, the trueness of His character, and hence the truth of His Word, are at stake. Here if anywhere, it is critically important that we speak the truth in love, compromising neither the truth nor the love. In the fundamental sense that they both proceed from His character, you cannot have one without the other.

Thesis 5: Apologetics, like every other aspect of evangelism, is impotent apart from the convicting power of the Holy Spirit; and that is a reason to *do* it, not to avoid it.

---

³ C. S. Lewis, *The Lion, the Witch, and the Wardrobe* (NY: HarperCollins, 1978), 52.

⁴ If you question the universal validity of the law of non-contradiction, try to construct an imaginary world in which contradictory propositions about the same subject can both be true in the same way, at the same time, and at the same place. You will not succeed. Your world will un-world itself.

Every person I know of who objects to apologetics as unspiritual makes the point that "You cannot argue people into the kingdom." They sometimes add the claim that nobody has ever been saved as a result of apologetic argument. Well, the second claim is demonstrably false. C. S. Lewis attributed his own conversion to the apologetic argument of J. R. R. Tolkien that, when Lewis rejected Christ as a myth parallel to the dying god myth of many pagan religions, he was being inconsistent. What if the dying god had actually happened once?[5] Charles Colson famously attributed his own conversion to the arguments in Lewis's *Mere Christianity*, and countless others give Lewis's arguments a role in either their coming to faith or their preservation and maintenance in faith.[6] It is certainly true that argument *alone* never converted anybody; but that is a very different claim indeed, and one that no apologist need fear.

The first claim—that you cannot argue people into the kingdom—is definitely true. It is also irrelevant. You cannot preach or witness people into the kingdom either, but nobody advocates the abolition of sermons or the repeal of the Great Commission on that ground. Only the Holy Spirit can bring a person through real conviction of sin to saving faith in Christ, and He has ordained

---

[5] C. S. Lewis, *They Stand Together: The Letters of C. S. Lewis to Arthur Greeves*, ed. Walter Hooper (NY: MacMillan, 1979), pp. 427–8. For more information on Lewis's conversion and the role of argument in it, see Roger Lancelyn Green and Walter Hooper, *C. S. Lewis: A Biography* (NY: Harcourt, Brace, Jovanovich, 1974), pp. 101–118, George Sayer, *Jack: A Life of C. S. Lewis* (Wheaton: Crossway, 1994), pp. 217–31, Alister McGrath, *C. S. Lewis: A Life* (Carol Stream, Il.: Tyndale House, 2013), pp. 131–159 (especially important for dating), Donald T. Williams, "G. K. Chesterton, *The Everlasting Man*," in *C. S. Lewis's List: the Ten Books that Influenced Him Most*, ed. David and Susan Werther (NY: Bloomsbury, 2015), pp. 31–48, and most importantly Lewis's autobiography, *Surprised by Joy: The shape of My Early Life* (NY: Harcourt, Brace,& World, 1955).

[6] For an evaluation of Lewis's apologetic, see Donald T. Williams, *Deeper Magic: The Theology Behind the Writings of C. S. Lewis* (Baltimore: Square Halo Books, 2016), pp. 216–32.

certain means through which He normally works in doing so.[7] If we let the New Testament tell us what those means are, we will have to include the written Word, the preached Word, personal testimony, prayer—and apologetic argument by people who have sanctified Christ as Lord in their hearts. None of the critics of apologetics have the ability to remove apologetics from the list, because they do not have the authority to cut the commandment in 1 Peter 3.15 out of the Bible.

No sinner puts his faith in Christ for salvation without a supernatural intervention by God. Whether they understand it as Calvinistic "irresistible grace" or Arminian "prevenient grace," all Christians should agree that without the aid of the Holy Spirit no sinner can be saved. The power of my preaching, the strength of my testimony, and the cogency of my arguments are not enough apart from that enabling. The Apostle Paul is very clear about this. "A natural man does not accept the things of the Spirit of God, for they are foolishness to him, and he cannot understand them, because they are spiritually appraised" (1 Cor 2.14). The natural man does not accept them and hence cannot know them because he is spiritually dead: "And you were dead in your trespasses and sins" (Eph 2.1). The sinner cannot believe the Gospel, whether aided by rational argument or not, without being enabled by the Spirit. It is not natural for him to do so because the Gospel undercuts his commitment to his own autonomy: It will not let him be his own Lord, nor take any credit for his salvation. Because as a child of Adam the natural man is a constitutional rebel against God's kingdom, he will not accept the Gospel on his

---

[7] For more on the role of the Holy Spirit in conviction and calling and regeneration and His use of means to those ends, see Donald T. Williams, *The Person and Work of the Holy Spirit* (Nashville: Broadman, 1994; rpt. Eugene, Or: Wipf & Stock), pp. 49–79, 210–216.

own. Apart from the intervention of the Holy Spirit in conviction and calling, he will remain in his sins. No proclamation, witness, or apologetic can overcome this resistance by itself.

All right, then: We are dead in our trespasses and sins and need to be brought to faith in Christ in order to be brought back to life. No preacher, witness, or apologist can do that. No wise preacher, witness, or apologist thinks he can. We preach, witness, and present evidence, not because we think any of that can be effective apart from the work of the Spirit, but because God has commanded us to use these means and promised to bless them and work through them. If we are faithful, sooner or later He will give some helpless sinner the ability to respond positively to the Gospel. Apologetics is no exception to this rule. The most brilliant apologist on the planet is just as totally dependent on the work of the Spirit to make his efforts fruitful for the kingdom as the most powerful preacher and the most sincere witness—no more so, and no less. We will be better preachers, better witnesses, and better apologists when we fully realize this truth.

Our absolute dependence on the Holy Spirit should not discourage us from preaching, giving our testimony, and presenting the evidence for the truth of the Christian faith. Most especially, that discouragement should not be focused on apologetics as if it were somehow uniquely unable to be effective without the Spirit's empowerment in ways not true of the other means through which He works. In fact, the logic should run in precisely the opposite direction. It is because we are absolutely dependent on the Spirit for conviction, calling, regeneration, and new life in Christ to come about that we have a reason to pursue Christian witness and pursue it apologetically.

If the new life sinners need were dependent on my eloquence, my earnestness, or my brilliance or persuasiveness (or Lewis's), we would all be lost. But because we have been commanded to preach, testify, and persuade, we persuade men, knowing that our labor is not in vain in the Lord (2 Cor 5.11; 1 Cor 15.58). We trust that God in His goodness and His love for lost human beings did not command us to speak and to persuade unless He planned to bless our obedience. We trust also in His wisdom, being granted to see that only when we give up all trust in our own abilities, having sanctified Christ as Lord in our hearts, do we have a chance to make arguments that can win people, not just debates; only then can we really speak the truth in love. And so we obey, and so we can obey in hope. And if we can do that, the Reformation we need and the Apologetic we need will be one step closer.

Conclusion

C. S. Lewis can help us in all five of these areas. He was certainly ready to give a defense, and he gave it at every opportunity, on the BBC, to RAF camps, in many books and articles, and in countless personal encounters and letters. Thus he shows us what it looks like when apologetics is an integrated component of Christian discipleship. He spoke to the whole person because he had overcome the modern dichotomies between head and "heart" in his own inner life with an insatiable drive for wholeness.[8] How many times have we heard someone say that the greatest gift Lewis gave him was just the demonstration that a Christian mind was possible, that the phrase "Christian mind" was not an oxymoron? He used at least six different arguments for the existence of God

---

[8] See Donald T. Williams, *Deeper Magic: The Theology behind the Writings of C. S. Lewis* (Baltimore: Square Halo Books, 2016): 14–18.

and the identity of Christ as His Son: the Moral Argument, The Ontological Argument, The Argument from Reason, The Trilemma, The Argument from Desire, and what I have called The Narrative Argument for Christianity. We will find each of them to have some validity; many have found them to be persuasive. And while they are intellectually rigorous, they are presented in plain language that one does not have to be an expert in the philosophy of religion to understand. Finally, one reason for Lewis's success is that he understood the necessity of dependence on the Holy Spirit for that success. In "The Apologist's Evening Prayer," he asks to be delivered from his victories, from his "cleverness shot forth on thy behalf," and from his proofs lest he be tempted to trust in them rather than in God Himself: "Take from me all my trumpery lest I die."[9]

C.S. Lewis was the greatest apologist of the Twentieth Century because of his great gifts, but also because he understood and embraced these five theses. As we turn to his actual arguments, we do so in that light. First is the moral argument for theism as it is presented in *Mere Christianity*.

---

[9] *Collected Poems*, ed. Don W. King (Kent, OH: Kent State Univ. Pr., 2015): 328–9.

INTERLUDE

ALWAYS READY: APOLOGETICS 101
Commentary, 1 Peter 3.15 in Context

[Speaking of the believers' response to persecution]: To sum up, all of you be harmonious, sympathetic, brotherly, kindhearted, and humble in spirit, not returning evil for evil or insult for insult but giving a blessing instead.... But sanctify Christ as Lord in your hearts, always being ready to make a defense to everyone who asks you to give an account for the hope that is in you, yet with gentleness and reverence. (1 Pet 3.8–15)

Somehow the hope within us must seem strange
  Enough to make it need an explanation.
  Our job: This situation to arrange,
  To stimulate a true investigation.
But how? The context is of persecution;
  The saints for evil are returning good.
  Why they would do that asks for a solution;
  On natural grounds, it can't be understood.
Blessing when we are expecting curses,
  Instead of hate for hate, surprising love:
  When one's assumptions meet with such reverses,
  One might just ask, "Could this be from above?"
Thus comes an answer hard to be ignored,
  When Christ is set up in our hearts as Lord.

CHAPTER ONE

A Clue to the Meaning of the Universe

C. S. Lewis and the Moral Argument for Theism

Introduction

In the dark days of World War II, Dr. James Welch of the BBC, having been impressed by Lewis's first apologetics book, *The Problem of Pain*, wrote to Lewis asking him to do a series of religious talks on the radio.[1] These "broadcast talks" eventually grew into the book we know as *Mere Christianity*. Starting from square one in trying to reconnect people with the Christian hope, Lewis began with the common human experience of trying to live with the inner sense that somehow life asks of us a certain "fairness" in our behavior, suggesting that this experience is in fact an important "clue to the meaning of the universe."[2] Lewis thus gave us a classic example of what is traditionally known as "The Moral Argument for Theism."

The Argument

The argument has three steps. First, it must try to demonstrate that we find ourselves subject to a moral law. Second, it must

---

[1] See George Sayers, *Jack: A Life of C. S. Lewis* (Wheaton, IL: Crossway, 1994): 277–80.
[2] C. S. Lewis, *Mere Christianity* (NY: MacMillan, 1943): 15.

show that secular explanations of this law—that it is purely subjective, that it is a result of conditioning or of culture, that it is a product of evolution—fail adequately to account for its actual features. Third, it argues that therefore the best explanation for this phenomenon is that there is a moral Lawgiver, that is, God. The argument will be persuasive to the extent that it successfully shows that a real and objective moral law exists and that the alternative explanations of it are indeed unworkable or inadequate. The advantage of it is that, if it is successful, it points to the existence of God in such a way as to highlight our moral guilt before His law. Thus it provides a natural segue into the presentation of the Gospel, the good news that this God has provided a way of redemption from that guilt through the gift of His Son.

Lewis brilliantly begins the first step, not with abstract ideas, but with a concrete scenario everyone can relate to: a dispute over some action—cutting in line, refusing to share, failing to keep a promise—that is deemed unacceptable.[3] People in such situations do not merely express their dislike of the act; they imply that it was wrong. It failed to meet some standard of fairness or rightness that is assumed to exist and to be acknowledged by both parties. (Curiously, even people who think of themselves as moral relativists will talk like this when faced with such a disagreement, especially if they perceive themselves to be the victim of the alleged wrong.)

Does this standard really exist, and do people feel themselves subject to it? Lewis asks those who question this proposition to do a simple thought experiment. Try to imagine a world in which

---

[3] See the excellent discussion of Lewis's use of concrete imagination in constructing this linear argument by Jerry Root and Mark Neal, *The Surprising Imagination of C. S. Lewis* (Nashville: Abingdon, 2015): 17–29.

people felt proud of cowardice or admired someone who stabbed people who had been good to him in the back.[4] To do this experiment is to realize that differences between the moralities of different cultures are more superficial than they might appear. Some cultures are monogamous and some polygamous, but they all recognize the institution of marriage. Lewis documents the common features of the moral sense across cultures in the appendix to *The Abolition of Man*, showing that there is indeed a sense of obligation to a universal core of common moral values across the human race that it is impossible to escape.[5]

Lewis concludes that virtually all people have this strange idea about how they are supposed to act, and that none of them always acts that way. He finds this odd, and he wants us to ask where this standard came from. And he promises that the answers explored in the following chapters will be a clue to the meaning of the universe.[6]

In chapter 2, Lewis starts dealing with what he calls "objections." These are essentially attempts to explain this moral law (or "natural law") in secular terms. If they are successful, then there is no need to appeal to a supernatural explanation. So we have entered step two of the argument as we outlined it above. Lewis deals with three common attempts to provide a secular account. First, what if the moral sense is really just an instinct, say, the human race's herd instinct? This would be a way of attributing it to evolution. What if it is really just a social convention, like shaking hands? This would be a way of reducing it to a part of our culture. And what if it simply a form of utilitarianism, a calculation of

---

[4] *Mere Christianity*, op. cit., 19.
[5] C.S. Lewis, *The Abolition of Man* (NY: MacMillan, 1947): 95–121.
[6] *Mere Christianity*, op. cit., 17–21.

what kind of behavior would benefit the human race as a whole? Here the moral sense would be really just a form of enlightened self-interest. Lewis tries to show that each of these explanations ultimately fails to explain.

The theory that the moral sense is an instinct founders on the fact that an instinct is not an obligation. It is a strong innate desire to behave in a certain way. But that is not the same thing as a sense that one *ought* to behave in that way. This becomes obvious when two of our actual instincts come into conflict. Seeing a person in a dangerous situation (say, a person who is drowning) might trigger a desire to help, which might indeed be from our herd instinct. But there might also be a desire to stay clear of the situation, stemming from the instinct for self-preservation. But Lewis points out that there may well be a third impulse, an inner voice that tells us we *ought* to obey the instinct to help and ignore the instinct to stay clear. That voice is not an instinct like the first two at all, but something else that judges between them.[7] It is the part of us that is in touch with the moral law.

The second theory, that the moral sense is really just a social convention, something we picked up from our parents, is given plausibility by the fact that there are many aspects of our culture that we learned from our parents or others, and which might be very different if we had had other parents and teachers. Westerners greet each other by shaking hands, Orientals by bowing, French people by kissing each other on the cheek. Such customs are important, but they are not moral absolutes; they might have been different and would have been different if we had been raised in a different country. Are moral laws anything more than that?

---

[7] Ibid., 22–3.

Yes, they may well be, says Lewis. Just because you learned something does not mean that people just made it up and could have made it differently. We all learned things like the multiplication table or the periodic table of the elements in school. It does not follow that they are arbitrary human inventions that could be different in other cultures. Well, is the moral law like shaking hands, or is it like the multiplication table? Lewis gives two reason why it belongs in the second class. First, the differences between the moralities of various cultures are not as great as people think. They are best interpreted as variations on a common theme. More importantly, cultural relativism as an account of morality leads to an absurdity: It would remove any grounds for opposition to evils such as the holocaust. If the morality of the Allies was more true than that of the Nazis, then "there must be something—some Real Morality—for them to be true about."[8]

The passage of time may have rendered Lewis's example less potent for us than it was for his original audience, who lived in the very throes of the Second World War. If so, simply substitute the morals of ISIS or Al Qaeda, which make a virtue of killing and even torturing people who do not believe in radical Islam. (This does not, by the way, contradict Lewis's point about the universality of the moral law. It is that very universality that makes aberrations like these stand out. Without it, they would not be aberrations, and our justification for treating them as such would disappear.) Giving up the moral right to be opposed to terrorism is a high price to pay for clinging to the comfort of cultural relativism. It is in fact a price people are willing to pay only in theory. Can you recall the days after the terrorist attacks of 9/11? Moral relativism virtually disappeared from America for about

---

[8] Ibid., 25.

six months, before it then started creeping back in. No one being robbed or assaulted thinks that the actions of his assailant are only unpleasant or inconvenient. When actually confronted with them, we immediately know that they are *wrong*. But where does that idea come from on a naturalistic basis?

The third theory, that the moral sense is simply pragmatism, that we accept these rules because we think it generally pays us to do so, certainly makes sense up to a point. We do indeed see that it is to our advantage to live in a society where murder and theft are not common. We can hardly be safe or happy otherwise. And so we agree to the rules and (mostly) follow them ourselves. But this theory fails to answer the most basic question of all: *Why* should we follow the rules that are beneficial to society as a whole in a situation where we think we would personally benefit from breaking them and think we could get away with it? Why *should* we follow the rules in such a situation? Morality reduced to utilitarianism quickly ceases to be morality at all.[9] It practically becomes a version of "Might makes right."

All three theories, in failing, have something in common: they utterly fail to account for the intuition of *oughtness* that is an essential part of our moral sense. As Lewis summarized this point in another book, you can juggle concepts like desire, compulsion, advantage, and fear (I want, I must, I would be better off, I don't dare) forever without getting the slightest hint of "I ought to" out of them.[10] An ethical system that can give you no reason why you should follow it is not much of an ethical system at all. *Ought* is etymologically related to *owe*. You can only owe something to a person, and you can only have an absolute obligation to an ultimate Person.

---

[9] Ibid., 29.

[10] C. S. Lewis, *The Problem of Pain* (NY: MacMillan, 1967): 9.

But we are getting ahead of ourselves. At this point Lewis has only established that secular explanations of morality cannot explain it. But he is finally ready to ask, "What Lies Behind the Law?"[11]

To answer this question, Lewis notes that there are two basic views of the universe: the impersonal universe of matter and energy is all that there is and it is just going on of itself, or there is something behind it that is "more like a mind" than anything else.[12] Well, the foregoing discussion of the moral law sheds light on that larger question because there is one part of the universe that we can see from the inside as well as the outside, and that part is ourselves. And when we look inside ourselves, we find two phenomena that are very hard to describe simply as cogs in an impersonal materialistic machine. One is reason itself (more on that in chapter 3). And the other is this sense of obligation to obey the moral law. That sense of obligation suggests that we are not on our own, and with the failures of the secular explanations, it suggests that something like a personal God makes more sense as an answer to the question of why it is there.

The last step is to see what else we can find out about this "something like a mind" that seems to lie behind the universe. The universe itself suggests that it is powerful (because the vast universe exists) and intelligent (because the universe is mathematically orderly and fine-tuned for life). But the moral law tells us even more, just as listening to a person talk tells you different things about him than examining something he has made. It tells us that God is fully personal, with moral character as well as intelligence, and that if these moral principles are as absolute as

---

[11] *Mere Christianity*, op. cit., 31f.
[12] Ibid., 32.

they would have to be in an uncreated, omnipotent, and eternal Person, then we are in serious trouble. Theism then is true because it is the best explanation for the existence of the law, and Christianity has the deepest recognition of the problem of personal guilt that the law creates and the most radical solution of it in the atonement offered by Christ.[13]

Critique

Lewis makes a good move in presenting the moral argument, not as a deductive proof, but as an argument to the best explanation. He offers the Moral Argument not as a slam-dunk proof, but modestly as a "clue" to the meaning of the universe. And certainly it is that. The difficulties in explaining the central concept of morality—its "oughtness"—on a secular basis, and the fact that the law makes more sense if we assume a Lawgiver behind it, are suggestive. They suggest that the existence of God is not an ancient myth that persists for illogical reasons, but that it can be seen as a hypothesis that makes sense of some very significant facts that are defining facts of human existence. If we find them confirmed by other arguments and by religious experience, then belief in God can be seen not as a delusion but as a reasonable act of intelligence. It is reasonable to conclude on this basis that theism—the existence of a personal God like the God of the Bible—is true.

The second step of the argument, showing the failure of naturalistic theories to account for morality, is where Lewis is often attacked. The charge is that he has committed the fallacies of False Dilemma and Straw Man by leaving out this or that naturalistic theory that is held to succeed where Lewis's allegedly weak examples failed. As Baggett admits, any such argument

---

[13] Ibid., 30–33.

"needs to avoid giving short shrift to any legitimate moral theory in contention."[14] But Lewis could hardly have offered an exhaustive critique of all such theories. What he did instead was to give us representative examples of such theories and show the lines along which refutations of them could be successfully attempted. He "sketches... the first steps" in doing so."[15] If the examples are indeed representative and if we realize that Lewis is only getting us started in dealing with them, then his summary of this step in the argument can be seen as quite successful.

I think, however, that Lewis's final step is actually the weakest one. The bridge Lewis tries to build from theism to Christianity is based on the answer Christianity gives to the problem of guilt raised by the moral argument. Lewis is insightful here. But just because Christianity theoretically offers a radical solution to the problem of moral guilt, it does not follow that it is true or that this solution is there for us. This weakness results from Lewis's deciding to stick with the Moral Argument which is his topic in the first part of *Mere Christianity*. For, like all the classical arguments, the Moral Argument can suggest that theism is true but cannot *of itself* establish that the God of the Bible is the One who exists or that Jesus is His Son. It would have been better if Lewis had explicitly acknowledged here what we realize from other writings that he knew was the case: that in order to nail down the Christian faith as the one to which the Moral Argument points, we would need to supplement it with other arguments. Lewis's Trilemma[16] and the historical argument for

---

[14] David Baggett, "Pro: The Moral Argument is Convincing," *C. S. Lewis's Christian Apologetics: Pro and Con*, ed. Gregory Bassham. (Leiden: Rodopi, 2015): 132.

[15] Ibid.

[16] See chapter 4.

the resurrection of Christ[17] are required to take the theoretical bridge Lewis gives us here and add steel and concrete to it so that traffic can cross it.

What have Lewis's critics said about his use of the Moral Argument? John Beversluis is a representative example. He argues that Lewis's refutation of moral subjectivism is vitiated by the fact that he treats it as a single genus, when actually "there are more sophisticated and nuanced versions that... cannot be disposed of so easily."[18] The example we are offered is Hume's theory of morals as based on human feeling, which Beversluis claims is not susceptible to Lewis's "loose-cannon generalizations."[19] Hume argues, "The notion of morals implies some sentiment common to all mankind, which recommends the same object to general approbation and makes every man, or most men, agree in the same opinion or decision concerning it."[20] As Beversluis summarizes it, in Hume's theory of ethics, morality is "a completely human enterprise... based on dispositions that have evolved over a long period of time, have taken deep root in human nature, and are all but universal."[21] If Hume's explanation is plausible, Beversluis argues, then there is no reason to accept Lewis's contention that accounts of morality that lack a divine moral Lawgiver fail to account for the essence and reality of morality. And if that is the case, then his whole argument for theism becomes moot.

---

[17] See Donald T. Williams, *The Young Christian's Survival Guide: Common Questions Young Christians are Asked about God, the Bible, and the Christian Faith Answered* (Cambridge, OH: Christian Publishing House, 2019): chapters 1 and 7. See also Frank Morison, *Who Moved the Stone?* (Downers Grove, Il.: Inter Varsity Press, n.d.).

[18] John Beversluis, *C. S. Lewis and the Search for Rational Religion*, revised and updated (Amherst, NY: Prometheus Books, 2007): 83.

[19] Ibid., 87.

[20] Ibid., 84.

[21] Ibid.

Well, I think Hume's theory is very susceptible to Lewis's critique. In fact, I think it can be doubted whether Hume's view is properly a theory of ethics at all, as it has absolutely no answer to Lewis's charge that subjectivist ethics is unable to account for the word "ought." That is, it offers an account of where moral feeling or sentiments might have come from, but this account gives us no reason why we ought to follow them. Why should I care that most other human beings have come to think of the act I want to do as wrong? Thus Hume is precisely susceptible to Lewis's charge that subjectivist ethics leaves us in the absurd position of having no moral grounds for our opposition to the Holocaust. His theory of sentiment is just a fancier way of way of leaving us in a position where might makes right.

Beversluis thinks Lewis is guilty of a False Dilemma because he does not explicitly refute every single version of subjectivist ethics that has ever been proposed. But when the philosophical jargon is stripped away from the allegedly "more nuanced" views, it is not clear at all that Beversluis has made his charge of False Dilemma stick. Rather, I would say, he just muddies the water. The other forms of subjectivism remain species of the genus, and they lead to the same place. In my judgment, after everything Beversluis can do, the superiority of God as an explanation for the moral sense of human beings still stands.

Other attempts to provide a naturalistic basis for morality, such as Wielenberg's,[22] fall prey to a similar problem. Such theorists think that all they need to do is produce a plausible natural explanation of how moral sentiments might have arisen. But when they have done so, they fail to notice that even if their sce-

---

[22] Erik J. Weilenberg, "Con: A Critique of the Moral Argument," *C. S. Lewis's Christian Apologetics: Pro and Con*, Ed. Gregory Bassham (Leiden: Rodopi, 2015): 141–51.

nario is true, it fails to account for why we should follow these sentiments. Lewis's best insight then may have been his focus on "oughtness" as the central concept in the whole discussion.

Application

Lewis shows us that the Moral Argument gives us a good reason for thinking that God exists: the Moral Lawgiver is the only explanation for the existence of the moral law that can account for its central feature, its "oughtness." He also shows us some useful things about how to use that argument. His use of concrete examples, his focus on the key role of the concept of oughtness, and his example getting us started in dealing with alternative theories are all features we need to incorporate in our own apologetic. Two major issues deserve further thought as we think of applying that example in our own times.

First, the relativism and the subjectivism that Lewis was already dealing with have developed more virulent strains than even he could have anticipated eighty years ago. One glaring statement stands out as a sign of how much things have changed. "The other man very seldom replies, 'To hell with your standard.'"[23] That is not an unlikely response at all anymore. Respect for traditional morality in general is at a low ebb, and the seemingly sudden shift in the definition of marriage calls into question the very universality of the moral law as Lewis defended it. Movements such as identity politics and multiculturalism encourage people to focus on differences rather than on what we have in common. People wonder if there is even any common humanity left in our national consciousness that can be appealed to.

---

[23] *Mere Christianity*, op. cit., 17.

We cannot then make one assumption about our audience that Lewis could still afford to make about his. But does this shift overturn his point? It does not, for two reasons. First, if we look at the whole history of the human race rather than simply accepting that the last decade or so in the West is as normal as it has come to seem, we realize how abnormal our own little slice of time is. Until very recently the traditional definition of marriage as a covenant between one man and one woman was widely accepted even if not always practiced. There have always been aberrations from the norm, and we are living in one. To attend to the larger sampling of data is to realize that our own moment, far from being normal, is the exception that proves the rule.

Second, Lewis himself showed us the way to deal with those who say, "To hell with your standard." People who say that always say it very selectively. The moment they or someone they care about is the victim of a breach of the moral law, their relativism shows itself to be the copout which is all it is capable of being. "Whenever you find a man who says he does not believe in a real Right and Wrong, you will find the same man going back on this a moment later."[24] In the same way, adherents of identity politics can only make a case for the unjust way in which they think their favored group has been victimized by appealing to what Lewis called "the Tao," the universal standard of right behavior that all eventually must recognize. Lewis already realized that for some people in the modern world an extra step in the argument would be needed, and he showed us how to take it. Today we will need it more often and may have to spend more time and effort to make it. But Lewis has already shown us the way.

---

[24] Ibid., 19.

The second issue that requires thought is the step in the Moral Argument that demands the most work: that of eliminating competing explanations, undermining the plausibility of attempts to explain the moral law on a naturalistic basis. Unfortunately, such explanations are like the Tie Fighters in Star Wars: "There's too many of them!" Fortunately, there aren't enough of them to keep us from blowing up the Death Star.

We must be prepared to encounter any number of such theories, and we must remember that Lewis's handling of three representative examples in *Mere Christianity* was only getting us started in dealing with them. But he got us off on the right foot. We must not assume that we can refute all such theories merely by repeating Lewis's examples. But we should also follow him by focusing on the issue of oughtness. Plausible theories about how all-but-universal moral sentiments could have arisen are not necessarily good explanations of how the oughtness of the law can attach to them. And, failing to account for that, they have failed to account for the very essence of morality.

Finally, we should follow Lewis's example in one more way— one we cannot see while we are inside the material on The Moral Argument itself. That is, it is one we will not realize he followed until we have read more of him than the section where he gives The Moral Argument. That argument will serve us best if we see it in the context of the other major arguments such as The Trilemma, The Argument from Reason, and The Argument from Desire. Some of them will confirm its suggestion that a God very like the God of the Bible must exist, and others will make the bridge from theism to Christianity stronger and more able to bear the traffic we hope we can direct across it. And that will be the subject of the rest of the book.

INTERLUDE

SEHNSUCHT

When the fog obscures the outlines of the trees
    But breaks to show the sharpness of the stars
    And the blood feels sudden chill, although the breeze
    Is warm, and all the old internal scars
From stabbing beauty start to ache anew;
    When mushrooms gather in a fairy ring
    And every twig and grass-blade drips with dew
    And then a whippoorwill begins to sing;
When all the world beside is hushed, awaiting
    The sun as if it were his first arising
    And you discover that, anticipating,
    You've held your breath and find the fact surprising:
Then all the old internal wounds awake.
    The pain is sweet we bear for beauty's sake.

CHAPTER TWO

Anselm and Aslan

C. S. Lewis and the Ontological Argument

"We trust not because 'a God' exists, but because this God exists."[1]

"But who is Aslan? Do you know him?"

"Well, he knows me," said Edmund.[2]

Introduction

C.S. Lewis wrote his brother Warnie on 24 Oct. 1931 that "God might be defined as 'a Being who spends his time having his existence proved and disproved.'"[3] The jocular definition reminds us that we could easily get the impression from listening to the interminable debates on the subject that the first question of theology is whether God exists. But if theology begins from God's having revealed Himself to us, which Christians believe is the only way it *can* begin, then that can hardly be the case. God, having spoken the world into existence, and having spoken through

[1] C.S. Lewis, "On Obstinacy in Belief," *The Sewanee Review*, Autumn, 1955; rpt. *The World's Last Night and other Essays* (NY: Harcourt, Brace & World, 1960): 25.

[2] C.S. Lewis, *The Voyage of the Dawn Treader* (1952; NY: HarperCollins, 1980): 117.

[3] C.S. Lewis, *The Collected Letters of C. S. Lewis*, 3 vols., ed. Walter Hooper (San Francisco, Ca: HarperSanFrancisco 2004): 2:7.

it and in it since, would be in a position, were He so inclined, to one-up Descartes and proclaim, "*Dico; ergo sum*" ("I speak; therefore, I am"). Believers could say, "*Dixit; ergo est*" ("He has spoken; therefore, He is"). The Christian theologian therefore does not begin by asking whether God exists, but by enquiring into what can be known about the One who has already taken the initiative and revealed Himself as existing.

The "whether" question inevitably comes up anyway, though, for Christian philosophers especially, but for theologians too. It does so because we need to be clear about the grounds of our faith, for our own sake and for the sake of those who have not yet had the experience of being addressed by the revelation of God in Christ that we believe is objectively out there in nature, history, and Scripture. As an apologist, Lewis had to deal with the "whether" question a lot, and he gave in *Surprised by Joy* a detailed account of the experiences and reasonings that moved him over time from unbelief to belief. One might get the impression that the existence of God—as opposed to Lewis's belief in that existence—depended on those experiences and reasonings, rather than their depending, like everything else, on His existence. That would be a false impression.

Lewis understood that the answers to whether God exists depend on His prior reality, rather than the other way around. He shows this in his poem "The Apologist's Evening Prayer," where his "cleverness shot forth" on God's behalf and his proofs of Christ's divinity are portrayed as tokens, coins whose "thin-worn image of Thy head" should not be confused with the Reality they represent.[4] He shows it in the essay "On Obstinacy in Be-

---

[4] C. S. Lewis, *Poems*, ed. Walter Hooper (New York, NY: Harcourt Brace Jovanovich, 1964: 129; *The Collected Poems of C. S. Lewis*, ed. Don W. King (Kent, OH: Kent State Univ. Pr., 2015): 328.

lief," where the believer's relationship with God has an existence logically prior to and independent of the reasons he consciously holds for believing in it.[5] Those reasons are important and have a significant role to play, but God does not depend on them. The *whether* of God's existence, in other words, comes after and depends upon the *what* and the *how*.

The Ontological Argument

This relationship becomes clear in what may be the most misunderstood of all the classical arguments for God's existence, Anselm's ontological argument. Anselm began by defining God as that Being greater than which none can be conceived. He then argued that such a Being would have to exist necessarily, because any being we could conceive as not existing would be less than the greatest Being that can be conceived.[6]

A superficial understanding of Anselm has led many to reject his argument as invalid. Just because we can imagine something, however great, does not mean that it exists. Being the greatest thing I happen to be able to imagine is not evidence of existence. (I can imagine a mountain taller than Everest, but that does not mean there is one on earth.) And existence is not an attribute that can be added or subtracted so that a being is "greater" with it than without it. Thus, the Ontological Argument has a certain circular feel to it. These objections are sound as far as they go; but I think (and it appears that Lewis thought) that they miss the point.

I would argue that Anselm's ontological argument is best used not so much as an argument about *whether* God exists as a med-

---

[5] "Obstinacy," op. cit.

[6] Anselm. "Proslogium." *Basic Writings*, trans. S. N. D. Deane (LaSalle, IL: Open Court, 1903): 1–34.

itation on *how* He exists. (His disciple and biographer Eadmer seems to have thought so too; see *The Life.*[7]) God is not just some random contingent entity like you or me who just happens to exist, and who could exist or not. He is not just *a* being; He is the ground of *all* being. In other words, once you understand what God is, you must see that He *has* to exist. I exist (I assure you), but I don't have to; I could as easily not exist, at least not in this world. (This is a contention I will prove soon enough, though I do still hope to put the demonstration off as long as possible.) If I ceased to do so, outside of a very small handful of friends and readers (I fondly hope), the universe would not even notice and would pretty much go on as if nothing had happened. If, on the other hand, God did not exist, nothing else would exist either.

The point is that as long as you are thinking of God as some random being, a bigger version of you or me, who just happens to exist, or who might exist or might not, i.e., whose existence is open to question, you are not yet thinking of *God*. To truly understand who He is, is to see that He exists *necessarily*, unlike you and me. This of course entails that He exists in fact. But Anselm did not start with the open question of "whether God exists in fact or not" and then come up with a clever way of answering, "Yes." His point was that this is precisely what we cannot do. To understand who God is, is to see that the question never was open in that way; it is to see that either we start with Him, or we cannot finish with anything.

The practical application of this reasoning to "*whether*" apologetics is the realization that we do not say that God exists because

---

[7] Eadmer, *The Life of Anselm, Archbishop of Canterbury*, ed. with Introduction, Notes, and Translation by R. W. Southern (Oxford: Clarendon Press, 1962): 29–30.

He is the biggest thing we can imagine. He is in fact greater than anything we can imagine. (After all, Anselm did not define God as the greatest being *we* could conceive, but as the greatest that can *be* conceived.) All our imagined gods—like Zeus—are bigger versions of us, and so they could exist or not. And I have noticed that these are the gods that Atheists typically argue against. I am often tempted to say to them, "Congratulations! You have just refuted the existence of Zeus. Thank you for helping us dispose of that lame possibility. Now, let's get back to the topic of *God*." All our imagined gods—like Zeus, and the infamous Flying Spaghetti Monster—are bigger versions of us—gods who could exist or not. Yet we have a concept of a God who is bigger even than that. Where did we get it?

The God of the Bible is not the kind of thing we would have made up. When we project ourselves onto the cosmos imaginatively, we get gods who are personal but finite, like Zeus or Odin. When we project our abstract reason onto the cosmos, we get gods that are transcendent but impersonal, like Atman or The Force. Such are the gods—the idols—that we build up from below. But what if God's personal Reality were so strong that it could impinge on our consciousness from above? In a discussion of the Ontological Argument, Lewis wrote to his brother Warnie on 24 Oct. 1931 that "It is arguable that the 'idea of God' in some minds does contain not a mere abstract definition, but a real imaginative perception of goodness and beauty, *beyond their own resources.*"[8] They are justified in believing in God, not because they imagined Him (on their own), but because they could not have imagined Him. That is why the very concept of His nature, once clearly seen, carries its own conviction of His reality.

---

[8] *Collected Letters,* op. cit., 2:7, emphasis added.

Perhaps the reason the Ontological Argument seems so problematic is that it is convincing only to people who have already *seen* this—people who have been granted at least a faint apprehension of the Glory of God. Perhaps then its best use is not in trying to convince people abstractly of this reality before they have seen it, but rather in helping them to see it. It is to help them see why they need to try to grasp for the first time the concept of *aseity*. (The word means that God exists *a se*, that is, "from Himself" or "on His own." He is not like us. We exist *ab alio*, "from another.") The Ontological Argument might be able to do this more effectively if the emphasis in its presentation were shifted from the "whether" of God's existence to the "how." I think C. S. Lewis shows us one way in which this might be done.

Lewis and the Ontological Argument

Lewis used the Ontological Argument apologetically only once in his public writings, and it was in a rather surprising place. This most sophisticated of philosophical arguments shows up in a presentation to the least sophisticated audience: the children for whom the Narnia books were written. It is the debate between Puddleglum and the Green Witch in *The Silver Chair*. Describing the scene where Puddleglum stomps out the Witch's mesmerizing fire, Lewis wrote to Nancy Warner on 26 Oct. 1963 that "I have simply put the 'Ontological Proof' in a form suitable for children."[9] How is this passage a version of the ontological proof?

To answer that question, we will have to take a careful look at Puddleglum's speech. The Witch has been arguing that Overworld and Aslan are only a projection of the children's imaginations. She

---

[9] Ibid., 3:1472.

suggests that they have seen a lamp and imagined the sun; they have seen a cat and imagined Aslan. The Marshwiggle replies:

> Suppose we have only dreamed, or made up, all those things— trees and grass and sun and moon and stars and Aslan himself. Suppose we have. Then all I can say is that, in that case, the made-up things seem a good deal more important than the real ones. Suppose this black pit of a kingdom of yours is the only world. Well, it strikes me as a pretty poor one. And that's a funny thing, when you come to think of it. We're just babies making up a game, if you're right. But four babies making up a game can make a play-world that licks your real world hollow.[10]

How is this passage a version of the Ontological Argument? The Witch's reductionism could be taken as a rebuttal aimed in effect at the superficial version of the argument: Just because you have imagined Aslan does not mean that he exists. Where did the idea of Aslan come from? You just made it up, based on a projection from cats you have seen. Puddleglum's reply calls into question the plausibility of this explanation in a way that transfers the ground to what I have called the deeper ("how") version of the argument. The idea of Aslan, he argues in effect, could not have arisen in that way. It is highly unlikely that four children playing a game could have made up a world with a deeper rootedness in reality than the only real and solid world they had ever experienced. The final answer to a refutation of the superficial version of the Ontological Argument is to remember the experience on which the deeper version is based.

In other words, we have to get past the Witch's reductionistic empiricist epistemology (explanation of knowing) to an ontol-

---

[10] C. S. Lewis, *The Silver Chair* (1953; NY: HarperCollins, 1979): 109–91.

ogy (explanation of being) capable of giving us something to know in the first place. How can Aslan be based on the existence of cats when cats cannot even account for their own existence? Is Aslan derived from cats, or are cats derived from Aslan? Something has to be capable of giving reality to everything else, and in Narnia that is not cats. It is Aslan or nothing. And because Narnia is something, nothing as the source of its reality is not really a viable alternative.

This is a version of the Ontological Argument "suitable for children." Therefore, Eustace and Jill will not be basing their faith in Aslan on the rather dense unpacking of the logic of Puddleglum's argument that I have just attempted, but on an intuition of its rightness that comes from something even more basic: the fact that Aslan exists so strongly that His revelatory Reality is able to impinge on their consciousness with self-attesting power.

Aslan is of course a picture of Christ, the Son of Yahweh, whose name means basically, "I just am." The children have known Him, and because they have truly known Him they know that to do so is to realize the inadequacy of even saying that they have known Him. "Well, he knows me"[11] is a more accurate representation of the situation: It speaks of Aslan's ontological priority to everything, which is felt and shown in (and known by) the epistemological priority expressed in Edmund's reply. If you are thinking of Aslan as just a bigger cat, however much bigger you please, you are not yet thinking of *Aslan*. If you are thinking of Aslan as a cat of any kind whose existence is open to question, you are not yet thinking of *Aslan*.

The children, who have actually met Aslan, know this instinctively, and Puddleglum's speech reminds them of what they know.

---

[11] *Voyage*, op. cit., 117.

Their minds "contain not a mere abstract definition, but a real imaginative perception of goodness and beauty, *beyond their own resources*."[12] They know Aslan not as a hypothesis or fancy they made up, but as something greater than that, something they could not have made up, something so great that it could not exist just in their minds. They know Him as the God Anselm knew, as the One who exists *necessarily*.

Application

I used to tell my apologetics students that they need to know the Ontological Argument, but that its sophistication and difficulty, along with the great debate surrounding its validity, mean that they should be slow to use it. They might be biting off more than they can chew. Lewis's daring move in giving us a "version suitable for children" makes me question that advice now. I still advise using the argument with caution because it is so easily understood (I think misunderstood) as circular. But Lewis shows that it can perform a couple of useful services as we make our case for God and for Christ.

First, the Ontological Argument can make us sensitive to the fact that few of our contemporaries come equipped with a good understanding of who or what God is. It is discouraging to realize how many even of our fellow believers conceptualize Yahweh as merely a superior version of Zeus. But Yahweh differs from Zeus not just in degree but in kind. Zeus is immortal but not eternal. He is the son of Chronos (time); time was already going on before Zeus came on the scene. He is powerful but not omnipotent, far-seeing but not omniscient, the king of Olympus but not absolutely sovereign. Homer makes it clear

---

[12] *Letters,* op/ cit., 2:7.

that Zeus is subject to fate—he cannot reverse the destiny that has determined Hector's death at the hands of Achilles, however much he might wish to do so. Yahweh's very name, "I AM," by contrast, calls our attention to His existence *a se*. And that puts Him on one side of a line that separates Him from every other being in the universe. It is what gives Him all the attributes which we just saw to be lacking in Zeus.

The typical atheist does not understand this. He shows it by thinking that the question, "Well, then, who made God?" is a slam-dunk rebuttal of The Cosmological Argument (the argument that the universe, being contingent, needs a First Cause). In order for anything to exist, at all, something has to exist *a se*, on its own; that is, something has to just be there. Something must have always been there; there must be one thing without an origin. Why? If we start with a real nothing, an absolute nothingness, nothing at all, then nothing is all we can ever get out of it. (Arguments trying to derive the universe from nothing always sneak some kind of disguised *something* into the nothing while we are not looking.) So something has to exist *a se*. Not one thing in the observable physical universe is a viable candidate to be that necessary Being. Christians claim that God is such a candidate, and the only one. The point is that by asking who made God, atheists show that they have missed the whole point of the very argument they are trying to refute with that question.

The God Christians believe in is a more interesting Being, a Being with a better claim to be the ultimate Source of all existence, and a Being infinitely harder to refute than the infamous Flying Spaghetti Monster skeptics have created so they can have a straw man—er, deity—to argue against. The gods Christians and atheists are arguing about are often not the same god. We do not believe in the god many atheists reject either. They often have not even considered the One we are trying to argue for. Lewis shows us how the Ontological Argument, or at least some of the concepts we get from wrestling with it, can help us avoid talking past one another on that subject.

Second, the Ontological Argument as Lewis developed it for children reminds us that apologetics is not best pursued as a purely intellectual and abstract conversation. Reasoning about the greatness of God, by itself, is unlikely to move to belief a person who has no inkling, no personal impression or intuition, of His greatness and majesty. It is pointless to talk about a Being greater than which none can be conceived to a person who has never conceived anything greater than Zeus or Odin. And the Ontological Argument, as they clearly and correctly perceive, does nothing to support the existence of *those* gods.

To vary the metaphor: A mountain taller than Everest could exist (there is one on Mars), but simply adding incremental meters or even miles to its height can never take us to anything that can explain why there are mountains, or planets for them to rest on, or atoms to make them out of, in the first place. You would still have a mountain greater than which another mountain *can* be conceived: the mountain one meter taller than that one. But that is not what we are talking about. Yet we do not need a mountain higher than Everest or even than Mount Mitchell or Clingman's Dome. We just need to look at those mountains, not with calculation, but with wonder that there can be such glorious things as mountains at all. Why is that? What could it be whose glory they reflect? Hmmm.

We would not often walk someone through the steps of the Ontological Argument as such—though there are times in which and people for whom that might be appropriate and useful. But we would speak of God with a new awareness of the profundity of His true greatness and its roots in His necessary existence *a se*. We would not let people waste time attacking the existence, or thinking we were defending the existence, of a lesser god. And we would invite people not just to listen to our arguments but to be silent and let the heavens declare to them the glory of God who is there.

Thus the Ontological Argument, even if it be ambiguous as a deductive proof, can serve to bring to a level of insightful articulation the inklings of God's uncreated glory intuited from the majesty-in-contingency of Nature or granted in personal revelation.

Glory be to God!

INTERLUDE

THE SOCRATIC METHOD AT WORK:
Michael Bauman Teaching Milton

"The first rule: Don't trust anything I say
   (I might be speaking for the Enemy),
     But when *Truth* calls to you, you must obey."
The student body shuddered in dismay,
   With pens arrested in mid-note, to see
     The first rule: "Don't trust anything I say."
"For there is Truth, though narrow is the Way,
   And few that find it." (But they will be free
     If, when Truth calls to them, they just obey.)
"Do *you* think that, or is it just O. K.
   Because I said it?" This, persistently.
     The first rule: "Don't trust anything I say."
"And what *is* Truth? And what the Good? To play
   The game, you have to know the rules—the key—
     So when Truth calls to you, you can obey."
His every wink and word was to convey
   The simple skill of doubting faithfully.
     The first rule: "Don't trust anything I say,
But when Truth calls to you, you must obey."

CHAPTER THREE

Printing Error?
C. S. Lewis and the Argument from Reason

Introduction

One of Lewis's more interesting arguments is the Argument from Reason. It is part of his defense of the possibility of miracles in *Miracles*, an attempt to refute Naturalism so that the study of the miraculous could proceed. It occasioned perhaps the most famous debate Lewis was ever involved in, when the philosopher Elizabeth Anscombe attempted to refute it at the Oxford Socratic Club on February 2, 1948. People are still arguing over whether or not she succeeded. Lewis took her critique seriously enough that he revised the relevant chapters of *Miracles* in a second edition to try to meet it.[1] People are still arguing about how successful *that* was. We will try to bring some clarity to the situation here.

The Argument

The Argument from Reason rivals the Trilemma as Lewis's argument that has provoked the most controversy. He lays it out in the opening chapters of *Miracles*. In simple form, he argues that

---

[1] Compare C.S. Lewis, *Miracles: A Preliminary Study* (NY: MacMillan, 1947) and C.S. Lewis, *Miracles: A Preliminary Study* (1960; NY: Simon & Schuster, 1996).

if Naturalism is true, then everything that happens must have a physical cause. This includes our thoughts. Then your thought that Naturalism is true is caused by chemical reactions in your brain, equally with my thought that it is false. Therefore, as one chemical reaction can hardly make a valid judgment about another one, Naturalism cannot be true. If it were, we would not be able to claim that it is true. Naturalism is self-refuting.

Lewis argued that Naturalism undoes itself because it presents us with a view of the world in which thoughts are reduced to chemical reactions in our heads, which are happening there in obedience to the laws of physics and chemistry rather than the laws of logic and reason. But if this is true, we have no reason to trust the very rational processes by which we concluded that our thoughts are chemical reactions. If my thoughts are determined by the physical state of my brain, by the history of the atoms that randomly ended up in motion there—if there is no free rational agent who can see logical relationships between evidence and conclusions—then all thinking is undermined, including the thought that Naturalism (or anything else) is true. How can one chemical reaction be right or wrong about another chemical reaction? If my thought and the thought of the person who disagrees with me are both just chemical reactions in our heads, who is to judge between them? The only answer is another entity whose thoughts are subject to the same difficulty as ours. This leads us nowhere. Therefore, reason must somehow be transcendent, something that stands above deterministic cause and effect. To deny this conclusion is to deny your right to deny it. Therefore (to make a long story short), Christian theism can be affirmed without contradiction, but Naturalism and materialism cannot.

It seems to me that Lewis was basically right: You cannot have a philosophy that undermines the transcendence of Reason and the ability of persons to access it and then give reasons for that philosophy or claim that it is in any meaningful sense true.

What some may not realize is that the argument from reason exemplifies a basic pattern in Lewis's thinking, in his way of seeing reality in general, not just its relation to reason. The world is a big and wonderful place, and only belief in God as He is revealed in Christianity can account for that largeness and that wonder. If God exists, there is room for all the facts the Atheist accepts. But if He does not, it is not only God and the spiritual that is excluded, but even the Atheist's world has to go also. There is room in the Christian's world for the Atheist, but the Atheist's universe is not even big enough to include the Atheist himself.

This pattern is evident whether we look at the world from the standpoint of knowing, of meaning, or of morals. In the area of knowing, Lewis noted that "When I accept Theology... I can get in, or allow for, science as a whole.... If, on the other hand, I swallow the [secular] scientific cosmology as a whole, then not only can I not fit in Christianity, but I cannot even fit in science."[2] What of meaning? It turns out that Atheism is just too simple to account for it. "If the whole universe has no meaning, we should never have found out that it has no meaning.... If there were no light in the universe and therefore no creatures with eyes, we should never know it was dark. Dark would be without meaning."[3] In thinking about the world from the standpoint of its relation to morality we get the same result. Lewis wrote to Dom

---

[2] "Is Theology Poetry," *The Weight of Glory and Other Addresses*, ed. Walter Hooper (San Francisco, Ca: HarperCollins, 1980): 138–9.

[3] *Mere Christianity*, op. cit., 46.

Bede Griffiths on 20 Dec. 1946 that he had to give up using evil
as an argument against God when he asked how he knew that the
universe was evil. "Whence came the light which discovered this
darkness, the straight by which I discovered this crookedness?"[4]

In each of these areas the Christian has a view that explains
the world as we experience it in all its vastness, wonder, and mystery, while the skeptic must posit a world in which he himself (as
a significant, meaningful, thinking person) does not exist. Taking
the Atheist's world view seriously causes it to self-destruct. He is
forced to saw off the very limb on which he is sitting. The Christian on the other hand can believe in the Atheist's limb and see
it as attached to the tree. As Lewis summarized it, "I believe in
Christianity as I believe the Sun has risen, not only because I see
it, but because by it I see everything else."[5]

Critique

Elizabeth Anscombe was Lewis's most famous critic, but not
the only one. David Kyle Johnson, for example, is confident that
Lewis's argument fails to refute Naturalism. He uses a rebuttal
we have seen before and will see again. Like Beversluis as we
saw in the Moral Argument and Hinten as we will see in The
Trilemma, he accuses Lewis in effect of a False Dilemma: Lewis allegedly leaves out of consideration more sophisticated versions of Naturalism that supposedly are able to survive his attack. Johnson thinks there are forms of Naturalism that do not
reduce all mental acts to their physical causes. Property dualism,
for example, holds that only matter exists, but that matter has
two kinds of properties: physical properties and mental proper-

---

[4] *Collected Letters.*, op. cit., 2:747.
[5] "Is Theology Poetry?" op. cit., 140.

ties. Mind-brain identity theory holds that there is a one-to-one correspondence between brain events and mind events—they are simply the same thing. Johnson thinks that these views make it possible for "ground-consequent explanations" (i.e., reasons) to be ultimate explanations of thoughts so that Naturalism survives Lewis's charge of being self-refuting.[6] He therefore concludes that Lewis is wrong to claim that "reasoning cannot exist if Naturalism is true."[7] As with Beversluis above, the debate boils down to whether the alleged exceptions to Lewis's generalization are indeed legitimate exceptions. It is not self-evident that they are

When we think of the argument from reason, we think of the opening chapters of *Miracles* and of Lewis's debate over them with Elizabeth Anscombe at the Oxford Socratic Club. Anscombe basically challenged Lewis on a technicality: He had not sufficiently distinguished between non-rational and irrational causes of our thoughts, which he had said that we discount when they can be shown to have irrational causes. Brain chemistry is a non-rational cause, but the resulting thought does not *have* to be irrational. As we noted, Lewis revised the relevant chapter of *Miracles* in subsequent editions to try to meet Anscombe's objections. Philosophers of religion continue to argue about how successfully.[8]

Elizabeth Anscombe's major philosophical work has been overshadowed for many by that one event: her debate with C. S. Lewis at the Oxford Socratic Club in 1948 over his Argument from Reason for the self-refuting character of Naturalism in the

---

[6] David Kyle Johnson, "Con: Naturalism Undefeated," *C. S. Lewis's Apologetics: Pro and Con*, ed. Gregory Bassham (Leiden: Brill/Rodopi, 2015): 94–6.

[7] Ibid., 91.

[8] See Reppert, *C. S. Lewis's Dangerous Idea: In Defense of the Argument from Reason* (Downers Grove, Il.: InterVarsity Pr., 2003), who summarizes the debate and concludes, rightly in my view, that Lewis's argument is sound.

first edition of *Miracles*.[9] At least it was a pretty significant event. Lewis had argued that if Naturalism were true it would remove all reason for believing that Naturalism was true, because it would reduce all thoughts to chemical reactions in our brains produced not by the laws of logic but by the laws of chemistry and physics. He stated his objection to Naturalism by saying that we discount beliefs that have irrational causes. Anscombe replied that irrational causes can produce true beliefs. Well, they can: You can be lucky rather than logical. But does this rejoinder really refute Lewis's point? That question has received varied answers. While the debate itself was thought by many of those in attendance to be a draw, it led to Lewis's revising the third chapter of *Miracles* and softening its title from "The Self-Contradiction of the Naturalist" to "The Cardinal Difficulty with Naturalism."[10] The discussion of whether Lewis's argument (original or revised) is valid continues, admirably summarized by Victor Reppert.[11]

On November 12, 1985, Anscombe addressed the Oxford C. S. Lewis Society on her response to Lewis's revisions. A transcript of that talk has recently been published.[12] In it, Anscombe explained why she still had issues with Lewis's argument; but in doing so, I would argue, she actually reinforces Lewis's conclusion.

Anscombe correctly saw Lewis's argument as an elaboration of J. B. S. Haldane's, which Lewis quoted: "If my mental processes are determined wholly by the motions of atoms in my

---

[9] C. S. Lewis, *Miracles*, 1947, op. cit-24.

[10] C. S. Lewis, *Miracles*, 1960, op. cit., 20–35.

[11] Victor Reppert, *Dangerous Idea, op. cit.*; cf. his "The Lewis-Anscombe Controversy: A Discussion of the Issues," *Christian Scholar's Review* 19:1 (Sept., 1989): 32–48.

[12] Elizabeth Anscombe, "S. S. Lewis's Rewrite of Chapter III of *Miracles,*" *C. S. Lewis and His Circle: Essays and Memoirs from the Oxford C. S. Lewis Society*, ed. Roger White, Judith Wolfe, and Brendan Wolfe (Oxford: Oxford University Press, 2015), 14–23.

brain, I have no reason to suppose that my beliefs are true... and hence I have no reason for supposing my brain to be composed of atoms."[13] To explain her objection to this argument, Anscombe offers "an analogous supposition": "It makes sense to say that linguistic marks—that is, marks that are part of a language as they occur in a printed book—are wholly determined by the machinery that printed the book." In this analogy the marks in the books apparently correspond to Lewis's "thoughts," and the printing machinery to his "irrational causes" for those thoughts, which he thought would render the thoughts worthy of being discounted.

Anscombe concludes that "we wouldn't dream of saying" that the production of the marks by machines gives us any reason for supposing that any of the propositions in the book were either true *or* false. She sums up her argument with two observations: first, that the supposition that the words in the book are "wholly determined by... the printing machinery is true," and second, that this truth has "no bearing whatever on whether anything said in the book is true" *or* on whether we have any grounds for thinking so.[14] The knowledge that the marks were produced by a machine does not necessarily render them false; therefore, Anscombe argues, Lewis was wrong.

Response To Anscombe, *et al.*

The first thing to be said about Johnson is that he has seriously misrepresented Lewis's argument, at least as it has been developed by later thinkers like Reppert. The argument does not claim that "reasoning cannot exist if Naturalism is true."[15] Truths and

---

[13] J. B. S. Haldane, "When I am Dead," *Possible Worlds and Other Essays* (London: Chatto & Windus, 1927), p. 209; qtd. In Lewis, op cit., 1st ed. 22, 2nd. Ed., 24.

[14] Anscombe, op. cit., 16.

[15] Johnson, op. cit., 91.

reasons can exist in a naturalistic world. But can the individual thinker be in a position to know that they are true and valid? Johnson tries to answer yes by pointing to artificial intelligence, that is to computers like Deep Blue and Watson, which produce brilliant chess moves or true answers to "Jeopardy" questions.

Johnson admits that, being computers, they do not actually know or believe anything. But he thinks this is not a problem because they can produce "reliably true beliefs" without having any of the non-physical elements Lewis appeals to in human thinking. But how do we *know* that these beliefs are reliably true? Because non-computers—human beings—can check them, confirm that the programming is correct, and verify them using judgment and discernment. Without those human checks, the computers might well be producing true content, but how would we know this? For in Naturalism, those human beings are machines just as much as the computers are. The analogy has as much tendency to confirm Lewis's argument as to overturn it. As we will see with Anscombe's argument from the printing press below, attempts to show that a mechanical process can duplicate meaningful human thought and produce warranted beliefs have a tendency to backfire.

Are Johnson's proposed versions of Naturalism actually able to escape the dilemma posed by the Argument from Reason? It is not at all clear that they do. It is easy to make up a phrase like "supervenient properties" or "emergent properties"; but just because you have named something does not mean it exists. That is the fallacy of reification. It is not so easy to show how mental realities like consciousness and intention can "emerge from" or "supervene on" a purely physical substratum.

Can machines produce real thought? I must confess that I had to read the pages where Anscombe draws her conclusion several times to be sure I had not missed something. For while Anscombe's analogy is interesting, the conclusion she draws from it is simply astonishing. If the analogy is apt at all, surely it points in exactly the opposite direction!

Why? Because a moment's reflection will show that the marks on the page of the book are not in fact caused wholly by the printing machinery. The misrepresentation of reality involved in claiming they are so caused is, well, egregious.

I have published thirteen books before this one, so I know a little something about how this process works. The words in those books were not generated wholly by the printing press. (Neither were the words you are reading now.) They were generated by me (a certifiable non-machine), edited by an editor who was presumably also not a machine, and then agreed upon by me. The type (in the old days) was set by another human being following directions given by the results of the first process. It is only because there were (presumably) rational agents involved that the marks in the resulting books mean anything at all. If some of those marks are correctly interpretable as truth claims, whether true ones or not, it is only and precisely because somewhere behind the machines there was a *personal agent* volitionally *asserting* them *by means of* the machine that produced the physical book.

Think for a moment about what this more accurate description of printing means. If I thought a book in my college bookstore had been produced by printing presses without any input at all from (allegedly) rational and personal agents, I should have no reason to buy it or read it. It might by accident contain marks that formed propositions that in fact obtained in the real world—but that would give me no reason for believing them, as Anscombe rightly perceived. And that was precisely Lewis's point: If the universe contains *warranted* true beliefs (to steal a phrase from a later thinker), then it cannot be reducible to an impersonal machine. To claim that the thoughts occurring in that universe were produced wholly mechanically does not prove that they are false, but that was never what Lewis claimed. He claimed that it removes our warrant for believing them—including our warrant for believing the thought that they were produced mechanically. Therefore, Naturalism cannot be a *warranted* true belief; therefore, it cannot be accepted as true except by blind faith.

Lewis left himself open to the kind of quibbling Anscombe and others have offered by being uncharacteristically careless with his words. He originally laid down the rule that "No thought is valid if it can be fully explained as the result of irrational causes."[16] But of course *thoughts* are not valid or invalid; arguments are. He was closer to getting it right when he said that "No account of the universe can be true unless that account leaves it possible for our thinking to be a real insight."[17] We must not only be able to generate true statements, in other words; we must be able to *see* that they are true, as opposed to simply assenting to them, true or false, only because of our brain chemistry. Valid arguments would be one of the ways we achieve such seeing. Now, it might be possible for true beliefs to occur in a naturalistic universe, as some of the sentences in Anscombe's book generated wholly by the machinery of printing might be true. But could there be *warranted* true beliefs? That position is much harder to defend, and Ans-

---

[16] Lewis, op. cit., 1947, pp. 20–21.
[17] Ibid., p. 20.

combe's analogy does nothing to defend it. In other words, we can quibble about terminology if we like, but the general thrust of Lewis's argument was certainly sound. It can be attacked only by those who wish to wrangle about words.

Far from undermining Lewis's reasoning, then, Anscombe's analogy ironically actually confirms it. It does not finally matter that irrational forces can produce thoughts that happen to be true. If we are limited to non-rational (because physically determined) means of producing *and evaluating* those thoughts, we are never in a position rationally to assert them as true claims. The naturalist then can believe in Naturalism, but he cannot, logically and consistently with his Naturalism, assert that Naturalism is true. If the marks in our books (and the books of our brains) were put there wholly by the machinery of printing, we have no reason to suppose that they are true, or even that they were produced by printing presses.

Haldane and Lewis were right. Naturalism cannot be asserted as true in a manner consistent with Naturalism; theism on the other hand can be asserted as true without contradiction. This does not in itself prove that theism is true, i.e., that God exists. But it does show that theism logically could be true, while Naturalism cannot. My conclusion then is that Lewis was right and that he ought to have stuck to his guns and continued speaking of the "self-contradiction" of the naturalist rather than merely of Naturalism's "cardinal difficulty." Anscombe had pointed out a problem with the *wording* of Lewis's original argument, but not with its *substance*, even though she apparently thought she had done the latter. Re-reading Lewis's revisions to *Miracles* suggests that even he was not as clear about the difference as we can be now. The Argument from Reason is ironically confirmed by the very analogy that its most famous critic thought had refuted it.

Application

Lewis's Argument from Reason is a curious argument. In my experience, people tend either to see its point intuitively and immediately or have a hard time getting their heads around it. To help them get their heads around it, we need to be aware both of the initial attempts to rebut it and of developments that have taken place since the 1940s. Those who are capable of articulating their resistance to it usually take one of two tacks. One is to employ an argument similar to Anscombe's original response discussed above: Non-rational causes do not have to have irrational results. The other is to question whether Naturalism necessarily has to be a form of reductionism. People might be aware of more recent forms of it that try to avoid that trap by positing that the mind is an "emergent property" of the physical brain.

Anscombe's final attempt to defend her objection ironically helps us defeat it. We can ask people to imagine a scenario in which there actually are sentences created by non-rational causes: the book whose marks are indeed *wholly* generated by machines. Even if some of its marks turn out to be sentences, and even if some of those sentences avoid irrationality, has this process given us any reason to believe them? It is not enough that it gives us no necessary reason to *disbelieve* them. In the absence of any non-mechanical source for those sentences, belief in them is simply moot. Anscombe ironically helps us see that, correctly understood, Lewis was right about the unavoidably undermined status of truth claims in a naturalistic world.

Could the notion of "emergent properties" get us past this dilemma, as Johnson suggests? Emergent properties is a hot topic in philosophy right now.[18] The discussion can get pretty technical. The idea is based on the correct observation that when purely physical entities interact, they can produce properties not inherent in either of the original objects. For example, when hydrogen and oxygen combine, you get water, which has the property of wetness that neither hydrogen nor oxygen had as such when they were alone. It "emerges" from them. So the theory extrapolated from this observation is that maybe the structures of the physical brain are so complex that mental properties, including consciousness, can emerge from those structures, purely physical though they are in themselves. It is thought that this process solves the problem of reductionism inherent in previous versions of Naturalism.

The problem is that this is a gargantuan extrapolation. No one has shown *how* non-physical realities such as intention or logical inference, not to mention consciousness, can arise from the specific physical properties possessed by brain cells.[19] In addition, water is still a physical substance, even if it does have properties possessed by neither hydrogen nor oxygen. But thought and consciousness are not. The phrase "emergent properties" functions like a verbal magic wand that can simply be waved over the mind-body problem to make the reductionism that is native to Naturalism conveniently go away. The Socratic question, "How exactly do we get from *any* complex combination of physical

---

[18] For an excellent overview of it, see J. P. Moreland, *Scaling the Secular City: A Defense of Christianity* (Grand Rapids, Mi: Baker, 1987), 77–103.

[19] See Brandon Rickabaugh and Todd Buras, "The Argument from Reason and Mental Causal Drainage," *Philosophia Christi* 19:2 (2017): 381–99, for a response to a recent attempt. Cf. also Dwayne Moore, "The Argument from Reason and the Dual Process Reply," *Philosophia Christi* 24:2 (2022): 217-39.

states to the validity of logical inference?" is one to which I have never received a satisfactory answer.

In both cases, it is helpful to focus, not on the question of whether truth could exist in a naturalistic world, but whether *warranted truth claims* could exist there. It has to be truth that I can validly perceive as truth on some basis independent of what the physical state of my brain dictates. There has to be a way of judging between my brain state and that of the person who disagrees with me other than a third brain state that is just as dependent on non-rational factors as our own. Nobody has shown how *that* is possible in a rigorously naturalistic world. Lewis's discussion of this cardinal difficulty—actually, self-contradiction, if the naturalist insists on asserting his Naturalism as truth—remains the best place to start in coming to understand the great gift God has given us: knowledge and truth that are capable of having a basis and of being believed *on* that basis.

INTERLUDE

THOUGHT

Whence comes a reason's power to convince,
    Illuminate the searching intellect
    With sudden serendipity of sense?
No change of chemicals or elements
    Could equal insight, letting us detect
    Whence comes a reason's power to convince.
Electrical impulses give no hints,
    Yield nothing that could lead us to expect
    A sudden serendipity of sense.
A chain of neurons firing boldly prints
    Its trace upon a screen which can't reflect
    Whence comes a reason's power to convince.
By faith we must accept this light that glints.
    The eye can't see itself, cannot inspect
    Its sudden serendipity of sense.
A mystery much like the sacraments
    Whose grace unseen we yet do not reject:
    Whence comes a reason's power to convince?
From sudden serendipity of sense.

CHAPTER FOUR

Lacking, Ludicrous, or Logical?
The Validity Of Lewis's "Trilemma"

Introduction

No apologetic argument that C. S. Lewis ever made is more well-known—or more controversial—than his famous "Trilemma" (not his word), or "Lord/Liar/Lunatic" (not his phrase) argument for the deity of Christ. N. T. Wright observes accurately that "This argument has worn well in some circles and extremely badly in others."[1] And some of the sharpest critiques have come from within the believing community.

It is curious that an argument that has become a staple of popular Christian apologetics should be rejected as fallacious by many who presumably accept its conclusion. With not only the validity of a much-used argument but also the competence of the greatest apologist of the Twentieth Century at stake, it is time to take a fresh look at Lewis's argument and its critics. Can we still use the Trilemma? If so, how should we approach it? At the end of the day, how does Lewis come off as an apologist and an example to other apologists? We will try to shed some light on such questions

---

[1] N. T. Wright, "Simply Lewis: Reflections on a Master Apologist after 60 Years." *Touchstone: A Journal of Mere Christianity* 20:2 (March, 2007): 32.

before we are done. The Trilemma has attracted more discussion than any other Lewis argument, and it impinges on many other apologetic issues. For those reasons, this will need to be the longest chapter in this book. I hope your patience with it will be rewarded.

The Argument

First, let's remind ourselves of the argument itself as it is presented in *Mere Christianity*.[2] Lewis is addressing a person who says, "I'm ready to accept Jesus as a great moral teacher, but I don't accept his claim to be God." We note first of all that the Trilemma is presented not so much as an argument for the deity of Christ *per se*, as a refutation, a heading off at the pass, of one popular way of evading the claims of Christ. This, Lewis argues, is the one thing we cannot say:

> A man who was merely a man and said the sort of things Jesus said would not be a great moral teacher. He would either be a lunatic—on the level with the man who says he is a poached egg—or else he would be the Devil of Hell. You must make your choice. Either this man was, and is, the Son of God: or else a madman or something worse. You can shut Him up for a fool, you can spit at Him and kill Him as a demon; or you can fall at His feet and call Him Lord and God. But let us not come with any patronizing nonsense about His being a great human teacher. He has not left that open to us. He did not intend to.[3]

Many critics treat Lewis's Trilemma as original. But it is actually a refinement of a much older argument, the *aut Deus aut malus homo* ("either God or a bad man"), which goes back at least

---

[2] See P. H. Brazier, *C. S. Lewis: The Work of Christ Revealed.* Vol. 2 of *C. S. Lewis: Revelation and the Christ* (Eugene: Pickwick, 2012): 91–102 for a survey of other works in which Lewis gives a version of the argument.

[3] *Mere Christianity*, op. cit., 56.

to the Patristic period.[4] Lewis makes the dilemma a trilemma by subdividing the *malus homo* (bad man) option into two types of badness—mendacity and insanity—which are potentially relevant to the case of the claims of Christ to be God. Later thinkers have expanded it again to a Quadrilemma: Lord, Liar, Lunatic, Legend, or alternatively, Lord, Liar, Lunatic, Innocently Mistaken. In this chapter I will use the familiar term *Trilemma* to refer to the *aut Deus aut malus homo* (or "Mad, Bad, or God") argument in whatever iteration we find it, because it was Lewis's tripartite form that gave it classic expression for most of us.

Lewis's version of the argument involves the following steps.

1. Jesus claimed to be God. (This is assumed in *Mere Christianity*.)
2. There are three logical possibilities in the case of such a claim:
    2A. He was telling the truth.
    2B. He was lying.
    2C. He was mistaken (and hence insane, given the nature of the claim).
3. A liar or a megalomaniac (the relevant form of insanity) could not be a Great Moral Teacher.
4. Therefore we must either accept Jesus' claim or reject him as immoral or insane. The merely mortal Great Moral Teacher option is logically eliminated.

Note that one could go on to argue that (5) Jesus was not a liar; (6) Jesus was not insane; therefore, (7) Jesus was God. One could; many have; I might—but in the passage from *Mere Christianity* Lewis leaves it at (4). He is explicit about his purpose: "I

---

[4] See Brazier, op. cit., 103–26 for a survey of its use before and after Lewis.

am trying here to prevent anyone saying the really foolish thing that people often say."[5] Lewis does not claim to have *proved* the deity of Christ beyond a shadow of doubt, but only to have clarified our choices. Jesus was (A) telling the truth and is the Son of God; he was (B) lying; or he was (C) mistaken—and one cannot be mistaken about the particular claim being made (deity) and be fully sane. The only choice Lewis claims to have eliminated absolutely is that Jesus was simply a great, but merely human, moral teacher—for a person who is a liar or a megalomaniac hardly qualifies as a great moral teacher.

Now, the argument is surely presented as *support* for the deity of Christ in that Lewis thinks that the other two choices will be hard choices for most people to make, as well as choices that give inferior explanations for the full data of the phenomenon of Christ. But people could still make them. "You can shut him up for a fool...."The easy choice—that Jesus was a great moral teacher but not God—is the only one Lewis actually purports to have eliminated completely. How well did he succeed?

The basic problem Lewis's critics have had with this argument, even in this limited understanding of it, is their contention that it commits the fallacy of False Dilemma, the premature closure of options. Marvin D. Hinten uses it as an example of one of Lewis's alleged weaknesses: he "overlimits choices."[6] If it can be shown that there are other legitimate possibilities for how to understand the claims of Christ, it is urged, the argument fails.

The other possibilities suggested fall into basically two categories: first, the possibility that Jesus did not actually make the

---

[5] *Mere Christianity*, op. cit., 55.

[6] Marvin D. Hinten, "Approaches to Teaching *Mere Christianity*," *The Lamp-Post of the Southern California C. S. Lewis Society*, 30:2 (Summer 2006, pub. April 2008): 8.

claims attributed to him, or that, if he did, he did not mean them as the bald claims to deity for which conservative Christians have taken them; and, second, the possibility that someone could indeed be sincerely mistaken about his identity without being truly insane in a way that would necessarily compromise his views of ethics or his status and authority as a moral teacher. We will examine each of these categories in turn, and then look at an additional objection: that, even if the propositions of the Trilemma are probably true individually, their combined probabilities fall below the threshold of persuasiveness (the "diminishing probability argument," or DPA).

The Critique: Biblical Criticism

First, it is argued, modern biblical criticism does not allow us to make the naïve assumption either that Jesus said everything that the New Testament attributes to him or that what he did say has the meaning conservative Christians have always attached to it. Few believers are ready to sign up for the Jesus Seminar and question wholesale whether the words of Jesus as reported in the canonical Gospels are authentic. But believers do need to concern themselves with the fact that many secular people today will not begin with a presumption of their authenticity. Thus, Wright thinks that Lewis's argument "backfires dangerously when historical critics question his reading of the Gospels."[7]

It is equally common to question whether Jesus' statements really add up to a clear and unequivocal claim to deity. All that is needed to deprive Lewis's argument of its logical force is the probability that Jesus' words should be taken in some other sense. For some, Lewis's failure to consider such a possibility robs him

---

of all credibility. As Beversluis put it in his earlier book, "Lewis' view that Jesus' claims were so clear as to admit of one and only one interpretation reveals that he is a textually careless and theologically unreliable guide."[8] What are these other possible readings? Here things get a bit murky. It is apparently easier to suggest that a greater knowledge of, say, First-Century Jewish background would make such readings possible than it is to come up with specific examples. Thus, Beversluis: "Lewis's discussion suggests that all individuals of all times and places who say the kinds of things Jesus said must be dismissed as lunatics. But this overlooks the theological and historical background that alone makes the idea of a messianic claim intelligible in the first place."[9] How exactly a knowledge of that background would alter the nature of Jesus' claims is not made clear. The best Beversluis can manage is, "When they did dispose of him, it was not on the ground that he was a lunatic but on the ground that he was an imposter"[10]

N. T. Wright takes a different tack, appealing to the "strong incarnational principle"[11] which was the Jewish Temple, the sign of God's presence among his people. Lewis doesn't so much get Jesus' deity wrong as "drastically short circuits" the original Jewish way of getting there: "When Jesus says, 'Your sins are forgiven,' he is not claiming straightforwardly to be God, but to give the people, out on the street, what they would normally get *by going to the Temple*."[12] By not taking us deeply enough into First-Century

---

[8] John Beversluis, *C. S. Lewis and the Search for Rational Religion* (Grand Rapids, Mi: Eerdmans, 1985): 54.

[9] Ibid., 56.

[10] Ibid.

[11] Wright, "Simply Lewis," op. cit., 32.

[12] Ibid., 33; emphasis in the original.

Jewish culture (at least as understood by Wright), Lewis fails to give us "sufficient grounding in who Jesus really was."[13]

Readers willing to brave the technicalities of biblical criticism can easily get the impression that there is a solid scholarly consensus to the effect that we can't really assume that Jesus said everything the Gospels present him as saying. Representative is Frances Young's contribution to John Hick's symposium *The Myth of God Incarnate*, "A Cloud of Witnesses." Young takes it for granted that the New-Testament writings were produced by people trying to come to grips with the meaning of Christ and doing it in terms of their own developing situations in their churches. Few would question that picture of things; I do not. But Young draws from it the conclusion that the picture we get of Jesus is "the result of believers searching for categories in which to express their response to Jesus, rather than Jesus claiming to be those particular figures."[14] Thus, "The titles were attributed to Jesus by the early Christians and were not claimed by Jesus himself."[15] Only in John's Gospel are claims actually put into Jesus' own mouth as opposed to the mouths of his disciples, and John according to Young is not a historical account at all but a later meditation on the meaning of Jesus' life. If this conclusion is true—or is even as solidly supported by a real scholarly consensus as is implied—then the Trilemma would have great difficulty getting off the ground, with its initial premise (that Jesus claimed deity) being not only moot but incapable of ever being established.

---

[13] Ibid.

[14] Frances Young, "A Cloud of Witnesses," *The Myth of God Incarnate*, ed. John Hick (Philadelphia: Westminster, 1977): 15.

[15] Ibid., 17.

Biblical Criticism: A Response

Lewis's argument as presented in *Mere Christianity* simply presupposes that Jesus said and meant the things he is traditionally taken to have said and meant: It considers "a man who was merely a man and said the sort of things Jesus said." The argument is presented in the form, "Given that Jesus said and meant these things, this is what follows." To note that the initial premise is controversial in some circles is not a refutation; a refutation would require establishing that the initial premise is false, or at least probably not true. And this, as I will argue, has simply not been done.

Why does Lewis, though, make an initial assumption that does not appear to be one that we can actually afford safely to make? It was not because he was unaware of biblical criticism. It seems to me that most critics of Lewis have simply ignored the original audience for the Broadcast Talks that eventually became *Mere Christianity*: not college educated people but simple British laypersons during World War II. To bring up the technical issues of biblical criticism with that audience would have been a foolish introduction of questions they were not asking, unnecessary complications they did not need to deal with. With a more sophisticated audience, one would, of course, have to be prepared to make a case for the authenticity of the Gospel accounts and deal with alternative interpretations, because the truth of the initial premise is indeed essential to the argument. That Lewis knew of this challenge and was prepared to meet it when appropriate is proved by essays such as "Modern Theology and Biblical Criticism."[16] Kreeft and Tacelli also recognize the necessity of having a response to the critical argument; they expand the Trilemma to

---

[16] C.S. Lewis, "Modern Theology and Biblical Criticism," *Christian Reflections*, ed. Walter Hooper (Grand Rapids, Mi: Eerdmans, 1967): 152–66.

a Quadrilemma: Lunatic, Liar, Lord, or Legend.[17] Their divinity-claiming Jesus is not a legend because, they argue, the documents are too early to have allowed for a long period of gradual magnification of Jesus' reputation by later followers.

Beversluis in 1985 rejected this defense: "When Lewis... justifies the popular approach on the ground that 'if you are allowed to talk for only ten minutes, pretty well everything else has to be sacrificed to brevity,' he presents not a justification but an excuse.... Why not write a longer book in which 'everything else' *can* be fully and fairly discussed?"[18] But here Beversluis falls prey to that regrettable tendency of reviewers to criticize the book they would have preferred the author to have written rather than the book he actually wrote. Would Beversluis have an audience of simple laypersons remain unaddressed? Does he really think it makes sense to confuse them with technicalities that do not trouble them? As for the "longer book," one could say that it exists in *Miracles* or can be reconstructed from various essays that do address different, more sophisticated audiences. In *C. S. Lewis's Case for the Christian Faith*, Richard L. Purtill has a fine discussion of that larger argument gleaned from a more generous sampling of the Lewis corpus, in chapters 4–5.[19] Most of Lewis's critics simply ignore that context.

In his second edition of *C. S. Lewis and the Search for Rational Religion*, Beversluis tries to respond to the arguments of Lewis and others that support a traditional reading of the Gospels as giving an accurate and reliable report of Jesus' claims. He says that

---

[17] Peter Kreeft and Ronald Tacelli, *Handbook of Christian Apologetics* (Downers Grove, Il.: InterVarsity, 1994: 161–74.

[18] Beversluis 1985, op. cit., 57.

[19] Richard L. Purtill, *C. S. Lewis's Case for the Christian Faith* (San Francisco, Ca: Harper and Row, 198): 45–71.

all such arguments "uncritically assume that the synoptic Gospels are historically reliable sources."[20] According to Beversluis, instead of scholarship, apologists like Peter Kreeft and Ronald Tacelli offer "a flurry of unscholarly pseudo-questions,"[21] such as why the apostles would be willing to die for what they knew was a lie. Beversluis claims that "real" New Testament scholars don't ask such questions because they "know" that none of the original apostles had anything to do with the Gospels. He says that "all mainstream New Testament Scholars agree that the synoptic Gospels are fragmentary, episodic, internally inconsistent, and written by people who were not eyewitnesses."[22]

For someone who claims to find fallacious motes in the eyes of others, Beversluis has a curious blindness to the beams in his own eyes. His whole argument here depends on the fallacies of *Ad Verecundiam* and *Dicto Simpliciter*. Even if all serious biblical scholars did agree with Beversluis, that fact in itself would not make them right. But they can only be said to agree by the sleight of hand of simply (and arbitrarily) defining a "mainstream" scholar as a skeptical one. Beversluis's unqualified generalization—*all?*— has never in fact been true, and is less true now than it has been at any time in the modern age. Richard Bauckham's magisterial *Jesus and the Eyewitnesses* is just one recent counter-example.[23] A basic source like Stephen Neil's classic *The Interpretation of the New Testament* could have provided Beversluis with many more.[24]

---

[20] Beversluis 2007, op. cit., 116.

[21] Ibid., 118.

[22] Ibid., 123.

[23] Richard Bauckham, *Jesus and the Eyewitnesses: The Gospels as Eyewitness Testimony* (Grand Rapids, Mi: Eerdmans, & Cambridge: Cambridge Univ. Pr., 2006).

[24] Stephen Neill, *The Interpretation of the New Testament, 1861–1961* (New York: Oxford Univ. Pr., 1966). For a contemporary scholar too late to be covered by Neill, see Lydia McGrew, *Hidden in Plain View: Undesigned Coincidences in the Gospels and Acts* (Chillicothe, OH: DeWard, 2017) and *The Mirror or the Mask: Liberating the Gospels from*

Beversluis in his revised edition also responds specifically to Lewis's own arguments in "Modern Theology and Biblical Criticism." He simply dismisses Lewis's point that people who claim to find myths and legends in the Gospels need to know something about myths and legends and his observation that source criticism when applied to modern authors where it can be checked is almost always wrong. Beversluis patronizes these concerns as "The Argument from Personal Incredulity."[25] Nevertheless, Lewis's incredulity is not just a rhetorical ploy but has very good and specific grounds in his claim that the whole enterprise of skeptical criticism is methodologically flawed—an issue that Beversluis just fails to address. But that claim is central to the case against this alleged "consensus." We will have more to say about this below. So far, we have to conclude that the authenticity of the sources simply has not been overturned by this argument.

The alternative interpretations of Jesus' claims are not impressive either. How is "When they did dispose of him, it was not on the ground that he was a lunatic but on the ground that he was an imposter"[26] a problem? "Liar" is one of the implied horns of the Trilemma. Isn't an imposter just one form of liar? Isn't Liar at least as incompatible with Great Moral Teacher as Lunatic? And N. T. Wright seems to expect of his readers a sophistication in modern interpretations of Jewish culture that even the Pharisees of Jesus' day did not manifest. After Jesus' declaration that the sins of the paralytic were forgiven prior to his healing, they were not in fact saying what Wright thinks they should have said: "Who is this who speaks blasphemies? Where

---

Literary Devices (Tampa: DeWard, 2019). McGrew makes a rigorous case for the Gospels, including John, as providing generally reliable and straightforward reportage.

[25] Beversluis 2007, op. cit., 123.

[26] Beversluis 1985, op. cit., 56.

can sins be forgiven but *in the Temple* alone?"²⁷ They were saying, "Who is this who speaks blasphemies? Who can forgive sins but *God* alone?" (Luke 5.21; emphasis added). In other words, Lewis's argument deals with the reactions Jesus' contemporaries actually made to him—not the one Wright thinks they should have made! Wright thus tempts one to apply to him Lewis's verdict from "Modern Theology and Biblical Criticism": These critics are so adept in reading between the lines that they have forgotten how to read the lines themselves.

Beversluis fares no better when he claims that all that is needed is to suppose that Jesus had been *"authorized* to forgive sins by God."²⁸ This again simply ignores the actual reaction by Jesus' contemporaries. *They* took Jesus' words as a claim to deity, and he did nothing to allay their concerns. In order to understand their reaction, as well as the significance of Jesus' allowing it to take place, modern readers might be helped by imagining the reaction of a radical Muslim Fundamentalist to a mere human being who claimed to be Allah. It is ironic that Lewis is accused of ignoring the cultural context of the Gospels' claims for Jesus by people who have obviously failed to make the effort to imagine the fierce monotheism of First-Century Judaism—a basic and essential prerequisite to any audience analysis of the words of Jesus! Far from Lewis's views of the Gospels revealing him as "a textually careless and theologically unreliable guide" to them, it would seem that the accusation would better fit Lewis's critics. Chesterton asked a pertinent question in his version of the argument: "Mahomedans did not misunderstand Mahomet and suppose he was Allah. Jews did not misunderstand Moses

---

²⁷ Wright, "Simply Lewis," op. cit., 33.
²⁸ Beversluis 2007, op. cit., 124, emphasis added.

and identify him with Jehovah. Why was this claim alone exaggerated unless this alone was made?"[29]

Young commits the same kind of fallacious band-wagon appeal to scholarly consensus as Beversluis, and adds to it a brazen *non sequitur*. Surely the New-Testament writers were indeed struggling to understand Jesus in terms of their own problems, as he says. This is simply to say that they were human beings. It does not follow that they put their own ideas into Jesus' mouth, or into the mouths of his close associates (like Peter in his famous confession), or that they manufactured incidents like Jesus forgiving sins, along with the reactions of those present. These are conclusions that would have to be reached independently, needing more grounds than the assumption that things must have happened that way because that is how "real scholars" understand the evolution of the New Testament.

That Young is imposing a concept of evolution on the New-Testament documents rather than reading it out of them is suggested by his strange statement that their "dates of origin span approximately three quarters of a century"[30]. First, that is very unlikely. The earliest documents are the first epistles of Paul, which are probably from the fifties. But most of the New Testament, including all four canonical Gospels, was already being quoted *as Scripture* by the Apostolic Fathers by the middle of the Second Century—meaning it had to be in circulation some time before that.[31] (And the Gospels are quoted by those Fathers such as Ignatius and Clement

[29] G.K. Chesterton, *The Everlasting Man* (NY: Dodd, Mead, & Company, 1925): 246.

[30] Young, op. cit., 14.

[31] F.F. Bruce, *New Testament Documents*, op. cit., 18–19. For the relevant texts see Michael W. Holmes, *The Apostolic Fathers: Greek Texts and English Translations of their Writings* (Grand Rapids, Mi: Baker, 1992) and for an English translation, Cyril C. Richardson, *Early Christian Fathers*. Vol. 1 of *The Library of Christian Classics*, ed. John Baillie, John T. McNeill, and Henry P. Van Dusen (Philadelphia: Westminster, 1953).

who lived at the end of the First Century.) The actual period of composition then may be as little as half what Young suggests, and his suggestion is hardly indisputable—but it is needed to give time for the evolution of the early Christians' understanding of Jesus that is assumed to have happened. And that is precisely the point. Included in the collection accepted by the end of the First Century are all four canonical Gospels and the undisputed Pauline epistles—all the major documents on which the traditional account of the claims of and for Christ are based. Even if later dates for a few of the disputed epistles be granted, the earlier dates we must accept for the rest make it all but impossible to posit the kind of evolution critics like Young assume.

Young is very honest about the source of the presuppositions that drive such an understanding: "The Christians of the early church lived in a world in which supernatural causation was accepted without question." But he says that such a world view is "unthinkable now," that "there is no room for God as a causal factor" in the modern mind, and Christian scholars, according to Young, must simply bow to that situation.[32] *But if we want honestly to examine the question of whether Jesus could have claimed to be—and been—the Son of God, that is precisely the point on which we have to keep an open mind!*

Young's closed mind, and that of his associates in the mainstream critical "consensus," renders what looks like textual scholarship an exercise in philosophy, determining in advance what texts are to be allowed to say. In this he is typical of the whole enterprise of negative biblical criticism. That is precisely why that critical consensus is unimpressive to conservative believers. It is philosophically prejudiced and methodologically flawed, not to

---

[32] Young, op. cit., 31.

mention actually counterbalanced by a significant body of criticism that, without the predisposing naturalistic bias, reaches very different conclusions. Recall Lewis's observation that the kind of reconstructive techniques practiced by skeptical scholars have an accuracy record near zero when applied to contemporary documents where the results can be checked.[33] I would argue, much as Lewis did, that Jesus' contemporaries, who were or had access to eyewitnesses, are in a better position to know what he said than modern experts trying to reconstruct the documents according to their own preconceived modernist philosophies. For anyone who looks at the critical issues in that light, the initial premise of the Trilemma remains strong.

In summary, Lewis's Trilemma did not, in fact, "backfire" with the audience for whom it was intended, even if it doesn't work with negative historical critics, a "failure" that Lewis himself would have expected. Even a more sophisticated audience that objectively examined the data would have to admit that the complications raised by modern biblical criticism do not overturn the initial premise of the Trilemma. According to the *documents* (as opposed to tendentious theoretical interpretations and reconstructions of them), Jesus in fact claimed deity: He made the statements and performed the actions, and He meant what He said. This is confirmed by the reactions his contemporaries actually had to those words and deeds.

Anyone using the Trilemma today should be prepared to make the case that Jesus actually made the claims whenever it is needed. The wise apologist will not simply repeat Lewis's paragraph from *Mere Christianity*, but rather adapt it to his own audience. This will involve notations such as "Here be prepared to insert 'Mod-

---

[33] Lewis, "Modern Theology," op. cit., 159–61.

ern Theology and Biblical Criticism,' along with further updated arguments."[34] Unlike his critics, we should look to Lewis's other books and essays as evidence for how he himself would have used the argument from *Mere Christianity* in different contexts, and then follow suit ourselves.

The Critique: Mistaken Identities?

The second major attempt to show that Lewis failed to cover his bases involves, amazingly, the denial that only an insane person could sincerely but mistakenly believe himself to be God, or that such a mistake would automatically disqualify him as a great moral teacher. McGrath thinks that "The option that Jesus was someone who was not mad or bad, but was nevertheless *wrong* about his identity, needs to be considered as a serious alternative."[35] Along that line Beversluis originally asserted that "We could simply suppose that although [Jesus] sincerely believed he was God, he was mistaken":[36] not lying or insane, just mistaken. He elaborates, "If we deny that Jesus was God, we are not logically compelled to say that he was a lunatic; all we have to say is that his claim to be God was false. The term lunatic simply clouds the issue with emotional rhetoric."[37] In his second edition, he adds documentation from psychological studies of insanity to the effect that "delusional people are deluded about something... but they are rarely, if ever, deluded about everything."[38] Just because a person is deluded about who he is does not necessarily mean that

---

[34] Extremely helpful in responding to the "consensus" of negative New-Testament critics are Bruce, *The New-Testament Documents*, op. cit., Bauckham, *Jesus and the Eyewitnesses*, op. cit., and McGrew, *Hidden in Plain View* and *The Mirror and the Mask*, op. cit.

[35] McGrath, *Life*, op. cit., 227.

[36] Beversluis 1985, op. cit., 55.

[37] Ibid.

[38] Beversluis 2007, op. cit., 126.

he is deluded about the content of his moral teachings. Beversluis concludes, "The sober answer to the question is No, this is not the kind of blunder that only a lunatic would make."[39]

Well, the assertion that a deluded person is not necessarily deluded about everything is generally correct; but surely its application to the specific case of Jesus would take some supporting. No doubt people may be sincerely mistaken about a lot of things, even having to do with their own identity, without being necessarily insane; and they can be insane without being wrong about morals. But make no mistake: We are being asked here to believe that a person could be mistaken about the claim that "Before Abraham was, *I Am*," a person who was in a position to be familiar with the standard translation of the Tetragrammaton, the Old Testament name of God, and still be considered a sound thinker about morals (or anything else). Is this really credible? Marvin D. Hinten shows how such support might look. When he teaches *Mere Christianity*, he asks his class

> if they believe angels really did appear to Joan of Arc to say she was God's chosen instrument to save France. Half the class shake their heads no; the other (quicker-thinking) half simply sit and think it over, because they already see where it is going. None of them see Joan as insane or demonic, so if they apply Lewis's line of reasoning they will have to admit God really did send angels to Joan, which they have no intention of admitting. I then bring Mohammed into the mix, a man who genuinely seems to have felt Gabriel appeared to him with teaching from God. We discuss ways in which a goodhearted person could be genuinely mistaken about their [*sic*] role in life: an *idée fixe*, a hallucination, etc.[40]

[39] Beversluis 1985, op. cit., 55.
[40] Hinten, "Approaches," op. cit., 8.

Daniel Howard-Snyder has the most sustained and rigorous argument for the idea that Jesus could have been merely mistaken about being God. He admits that believing one is divine when one is not is believing something "importantly false," but then claims that "Merely being wrong about something important, even something as important as whether one is divine, neither implies nor makes it likely that one is a lunatic, insane, deranged, or otherwise fit to be institutionalized."[41] To support this audacious claim he tries to imagine scenarios in which Jesus could have had what seemed to him adequate grounds for believing he was God, grounds that, while seemingly adequate, turned out to be fallible—grounds that could be accepted by someone who was not insane. Perhaps Satan could have given him the ability to perform miracles and duplicated in his mind the subjective experience of being divinity incarnate. Perhaps Jesus, convinced that he was the Messiah, found exegetical grounds in the Old Testament for believing that the Messiah was in some sense divine. (This would be plausible because in fact the early Christians did find such textual arguments for Christ's divinity after the fact). For Howard-Snyder, these are "good but fallible grounds" that a person might have for believing in his own divinity.[42] Jesus might have made such deductions in error, or applied them to himself in error, without being insane. Howard-Snyder does not claim that either scenario actually obtains, but simply that their possibility makes it impossible to dismiss the "sincerely mistaken but still sane" option; therefore, the Mad, Bad, or God argument fails.

[41] Daniel Howard-Snyder, "Was Jesus Mad, Bad, or God? ... Or Merely Mistaken?" *Faith and Philosophy* 21:4 (Oct. 2004): 463.

[42] Ibid., 474.

Okay, so the argument goes, you can be mistaken about your identity without being insane. Likewise, you can be mistaken about your identity without undermining your views of ethics. Lewis "apparently thought that if certain factual claims Jesus made about himself were false, a disastrous conclusion would follow about the truth, sanity, and reliability of his moral teachings. But why say that?"[43] Beversluis goes on to ask, "Did Lewis think that if Jesus were not God, there would no longer be any reason for believing that love is preferable to hate, humility to arrogance, charity to vindictiveness, meekness to oppressiveness, fidelity to adultery, or truthfulness to deception?"[44] According to Howard-Snyder, we are not in a position to say that the diabolic deception or exegetical misapplication scenarios "are significantly less likely or plausible than the God option."[45] So the Trilemma fails at every point by this view. You can in theory be mistaken about your identity without being insane *and* without having false views of ethics; therefore, Lewis has failed to eliminate the "Great Moral Teacher but not God" view of Jesus and hung his apologetic on a fallacious hook. "Contrary to what Lewis claims, we *can* deny that Jesus was God and say that he was a great moral teacher."[46]

Mistaken Identities? A Response

Let us begin by remembering the conclusion of Lewis's Trilemma: that Jesus could not have been a great moral teacher but not God. The response of the critics is, well, why could he not have been just sincerely mistaken about being God without being in-

[43] Beversluis 1985, op. cit., 55.
[44] Ibid.
[45] Howard-Snyder, op. cit., 478.
[46] Beversluis 2007, op. cit., 135.

sane, or have been mentally imbalanced in some sense and still be a great moral teacher? So we need to be clear about what it would take to be a great moral teacher. I would suggest the following criteria: First, you have moral teachings that both resonate with humankind's most basic instincts about right and wrong and also state them in ways both profound and challenging. Second, you have to live before your followers with admirable consistency a life that is in accordance with your own version of those teachings. Third, you must be sufficiently in touch with reality that your teachings have general credibility. Clearly, if Jesus had been lying about his claims, he would be disqualified by the second test; but few accuse him of that. More importantly for this discussion, a person who failed the third test would also have problems with the trustworthiness needed to fully inhabit the role, even if he were not morally culpable for them. This is where the rubber meets the road in evaluating the claim that Jesus could have been simply mistaken about his deity.

Most of Lewis's critics succeed in undermining his argument only by use of a clever sleight of hand known as the Fallacy of Equivocation. The argument most of them are critiquing is simply not the one that Lewis made. Most of the criticisms deal with the *general concept* of mistaken identity, whereas Lewis is dealing with a very *specific case* of it, the false claim *to be God*. As Horner rightly puts it, Beversluis's representation of the case (if "certain factual claims Jesus made about himself were false...") is hardly adequate. "The factual claims in question are of cosmic, as well as supremely personal and existential, consequence."[47] Treating such

---

[47] David A. Horner, "*Aut Deus aut Malus Homo*: A Defense of C.S. Lewis's 'Shocking Alternative,'" *C. S. Lewis as Philosopher: Truth, Goodness, and Beauty*, ed. David Baggett, Gary Habermas, and Jerry L. Walls (Downers Grove, Il.: IVP Academic, 2008): 77.

vastly different cases of mistaken identity as equivalent is illogical at best and dishonest at worst. But Lewis's critics have to do it in order to make their criticisms sound plausible. (Howard-Snyder does deal more directly with the specific claim to divinity, but does not take it with sufficient seriousness, as I will try to show.)

This weakness becomes very clear when we examine the examples Hinten uses to support the claim that mistaken identity does not necessarily entail insanity. Joan of Arc and Mohammed thought they had seen angels and had a special role in history as a result. One can just imagine that they could have been victims of some kind of hallucination or had some kind of experience that they misinterpreted, and that this could all have happened without compromising their general soundness of mind or their views of ethics. But the problem is that such examples are simply not relevant to Lewis's argument. Joan and Muhammed did not claim to be *God*. That is, they did not claim to have existed from eternity in a special relationship with God the Father that made them Lord and gave them the authority to command the elements and forgive sins. They did not claim that they had a prior existence that was omniscient, omnipotent, and omnipresent—all of which is implied in and entailed by the specific nature of Jesus' claims. They did not claim that he who had seen them had seen the Father. *They did not claim to be the Yahweh of the Patriarchs and Moses incarnate in human flesh!*

How is it possible to miss the profound difference between all other mistakes about one's own identity and this one? One who wrongly believes that he is Napoleon has only confused himself with another finite human being. (Even this would present problems for the claim to be a great moral teacher. As Horner correctly observes, having correct views on ethics is a necessary, but hardly a sufficient condition for being a great moral teacher.)[48] As Kreeft notes, "A measure of your insanity is the size of the gap between what you think you are and what you really are."[49] Indeed, Chesterton makes a similar point: "Normally speaking, the greater a man is, the less likely he is to make the very greatest claim. Outside the unique case we are considering, the only kind of man who ever does make that kind of claim is a very small man: a secretive or self-centered monomaniac."[50]

Kreeft and Chesterton are right: To believe that one is Yahweh differs from all other such mistaken claims by an order of magnitude that is... well, infinite. It compounds a mistake of fact ("I am this finite created being, not that one") with an error in metaphysics ("I am not *a* finite being at all, but the Ground of all Being"). This is not, as Lewis's critics want to believe, merely a matter of degree. The gap between any creature and the Creator is a difference of kind.

One might object that, while the difference between the Creator and the creature is a difference of kind, the *claim* itself does not so differ from other claims, since all delusions are ontologically false to the same degree, that is, completely. But even if we accept this analysis and agree that all false claims are equally incorrect, it does not follow that all such errors are equally serious, much less morally equivalent. Falsely claiming to be Napoleon, for example, does not make one guilty of blasphemy. Mistaking one creature for another is an error, conceivably innocent; mistaking a creature for the Creator is idolatry. The error attributed to

---

[48] Ibid.

[49] Peter Kreeft, *Fundamentals of the Faith: Essays in Christian Apologetics* (San Francisco, Ca: Ignatius Press, 1988): 60. See his full discussion, 59–63.

[50] Chesterton, *Everlasting Man,* op. cit., 247.

Jesus would be of the latter variety, and surely not irrelevant to his status as a Great Moral Teacher—especially among first-century Jews! Anyone sincerely mistaken about being God would miss our third criterion for great moral teacher, being clearly out of touch with reality. Any first-century Jew so mistaken would run afoul of the second as well, being guilty of two of the most serious sins recognized by that society: blasphemy and idolatry.

To put it bluntly, therefore, Lewis's critics' ability to rebut his argument depends on their ability to substitute a different and inferior argument while no one is looking and get away with it. When, like Lewis, we remember the radical nature of what Jesus actually claimed and compare it with the ridiculously inadequate examples urged against the Trilemma, the attempts to evade its force become laughably absurd.

An equal lack of attention to what Lewis actually said appears in the attempt to evade his claims about the implications of the relationship between Christ's person and his teaching. Beversluis asks, "Did Lewis think that if Jesus were not God, there would no longer be any reason for believing that love is preferable to hate, humility to arrogance, charity to vindictiveness, meekness to oppressiveness, fidelity to adultery, or truthfulness to deception?"[51] But Lewis was not evaluating the moral truth of Jesus' teaching; he was examining the claims of the *Teacher*. His whole argument presupposes the self-evident truth of the teachings, which is part of the evidence to be considered in evaluating the sanity of the Teacher.[52] What is under scrutiny is the claims of the Teacher. Lewis is not saying that, if he were insane enough to wrongly think he was the omnipotent God, Jesus' moral teaching would be

---

[51] Beversluis 1985, op. cit., 55.
[52] Lewis, *Mere Christianity*, op. cit., 137.

refuted. He is saying that the self-evident truth of those teachings and their widely acknowledged superiority to all other attempts to state the same ideals refutes (i.e., is incompatible with) the notion that their source was a blatant liar or a megalomaniac. Nothing that his critics have said makes those propositions any more consistent than they ever were before. Beversluis's question is simply beside the point.

Howard-Snyder is an exception to my dismissal of the attempts above to show that mistaken identity does not entail insanity because he does try to deal with the specific case of mistakenly believing that one is God. Yet in reading his argument I cannot escape the impression that, having used the word "God" in one sentence, he immediately forgets in the next sentence what that word means. How else could anyone write with a straight face a sentence like this? "Merely being wrong about something important, even something as important as whether one is divine, neither implies nor makes it likely that one is a lunatic, insane, deranged, or otherwise fit to be institutionalized."[53] It is not so much the "importance" as the *nature* of the claim to divinity that calls into question the sanity of any mere mortal who makes it, and guarantees the insanity of anyone who makes it falsely. Indeed, some of Jesus' opponents, and for a while even members of his own family, questioned his sanity—not surprisingly. They had not evacuated the word *God* of its meaning, or the concept of God of its transcendence. Howard-Snyder rhetorically softens the nature of the claim even with his diction: the abstraction to be "divine" rather than what is at issue, the concrete and personal claim to be *God*. I repeat: it is the claim to have existed from eternity in a special relationship with God the Father that made a person

---

[53] Howard-Snyder, op. cit., 463.

Lord and gave him the authority to command the elements and forgive sins. It is the claim that he had a prior existence that was omniscient, omnipotent, and omnipresent. It is the claim that he who had seen this one had seen the Father. It was, particularly for Jesus, the claim to be *the Yahweh of the Patriarchs and Moses incarnate in human flesh.*

Howard-Snyder also confuses the issue by introducing the word *institutionalized.* The Trilemma does not require that a Jesus falsely claiming divinity would qualify for any specific modern diagnosis of a pathology justifying institutionalization; it only requires that he be unbalanced enough to be out of touch with reality and thus disqualified as a great moral teacher. Surely megalomania would suffice as such a disqualification? And surely the false claim to be God, made sincerely, would count as megalomania? If not, perhaps our requirements for "great moral teacher" have receded as far as our concept of what it takes to be God!

If we remember what it means to be God, then, we must agree with Stephen T. Davis that we are "not prepared to allow that anybody other than God ever has sufficient reason to consider himself divine."[54] Howard-Snyder's attempts to imagine scenarios in which a sane person could be falsely persuaded that he is God fail at two points. First, they again have forgotten the full meaning of what it would have meant for a devout first-century Jew to think he was God. Howard-Snyder realizes correctly that it would not be enough for Satan to grant the power to do miracles, because prophets were believed to have performed miracles. So he has to have Satan reconstruct for Jesus the subjective experience of being God incarnate. The problem with this is that no

---

[54] Stephen T. Divis, "The Mad/Bad/God Trilemma: A Reply to Daniel Howard-Snyder." *Faith and Philosophy* 21:4 (Oct. 2004): 491.

one who has not been God incarnate could possibly know what that experience is. Hence, we have to ask, how would falsely assuming that one is having that experience not be megalomania? Having Jesus conclude his divinity through faulty exegesis of the Hebrew Bible runs up against the same problem. Surely a *sane* person who understands the concept of God would conclude of any text that persuaded him that he was, contrary to all his experience, immortal, omniscient, and omnipotent, that there was a problem either with the text or with his reading of it.

The second problem with Howard-Snyder's scenarios is that, to establish the reasonableness of the sincerely-mistaken option, they would have to establish it, not for just any imaginable abstract figure, but for *Jesus*. Howard-Snyder lays down two ground rules at the outset: we must not treat the historical accounts as inspired Scripture, and we must not import into the discussion any independent evidence for Jesus' divinity, such as his miracles, teaching, or resurrection, etc.[55] Many apologists are prepared to accept the first condition for the sake of argument; few are prepared to accept the second. There is a good reason for this refusal. The purpose of the Trilemma is not just to establish some abstract truth but to facilitate an encounter with Christ by clarifying the options of how we can understand *Him*. And so the question is, for example, not whether Satan could persuade some abstract random person that he was divine, but whether it makes sense to say that he could so have persuaded *Jesus*. Does *Jesus* strike us as a person who had been so deluded, as a person under Satanic influence? Interestingly, Jesus had His own answer to that scenario: if He did his great works by the power of Satan, then that would mean that Satan was fighting against his

---

[55] Howard-Snyder, op. cit., 458.

own kingdom, since Jesus' works were clearly works of mercy and goodness (Matt 12.25–28).

In summary, the attempts to show that the Trilemma omits valid but unconsidered options all fail.[56] In order to reject Lewis's argument, you have to be prepared to affirm that a person in his right mind can sincerely but mistakenly believe, not simply that he has been visited by an angel, but that he is Almighty God, the Creator of the Universe, and still retain any credibility on anything else he might say. Since very few people in their right minds are prepared to accept that conclusion, most of Lewis's critics are forced to try to undermine his argument by sneakily substituting a straw man for it. Refuting that weak substitution, they then pretend to have refuted the Trilemma. But no reader who is actually paying attention should fall for this shell game—for that is what it essentially is. Howard-Snyder's attempt to support the sincerely mistaken option must be taken more seriously, for it does attempt to deal with the claim to be God rather than merely with the concept of mistaken identity in general. But it also fails by omitting to keep the full concept of deity in the forefront of our minds throughout the discussion.

Diminishing Probabilities?

Another attempt to find problems with the Trilemma does not attack its individual propositions but accepts for the sake of argument that they are each probably true. The problem is that when there are many such propositions, even if each is probably true,

---

[56] I have not dealt with them all of course, but only with the major and more credible ones. Another option—that Jesus was a new-age type pantheistic guru—is demolished by Douglas Groothuis in *Christian Apologetics: A Comprehensive Case for Biblical Faith*, 2nd ed. (InterVarsity Press, 2022): 551–2.

when the probabilities are multiplied together, the probability of the whole is significantly weakened. For example, if you have four independent propositions that are each probably true with a probability of .85, the probability of all four being true together is only .522—even odds, hardly a compelling case.

In the case of the Trilemma as Howard-Snyder analyzes it, you have to affirm that Jesus claimed to be God, that he was not lying, that he was not insane, and that he was not merely mistaken without being insane. If all four of these propositions are true, then it follows with deductive validity that he was telling the truth and was God. But all four are historical propositions, and therefore they are only probably true at best because historical investigation cannot yield mathematical certainty. And all four, especially the first, are contested. Howard-Snyder gives what he considers charitable and generous ranges of probability to each proposition, ranging from .7-.9 for the claim to divinity to .85-.95 for the others, and ends with a range of only .43-.77 for the whole.[57] Therefore, he concludes, we should "profess ignorance and suspend judgment about the matter" rather than claiming that the Trilemma shows it to be rational to believe in Jesus' divinity.[58]

There are a number of ways in which we could respond to this case. We could argue for higher values for the probabilities; but skeptics would have their own arguments for why they should be lower, and we would really just be arguing the case for the truth of each proposition, which we are going to have to do anyway. Never-

---

[57] Howard-Snyder's probability ranges are intended to take into account the possibility of probabilistic dependence among the premises. For more information on arguments based on alleged dwindling probabilities, see Tim McGrew, "Has Plantinga Refuted the Historical Argument?" *Philosophia Christi* 6 (2004): 7–26; Tim McGrew and Lydia McGrew, "On the Historical Argument: A Rejoinder to Plantinga." *Philosophia Christi* 8 (2006): 23–38.

[58] Ibid., 462.

theless, we have already argued that it is not necessary (or wise) to follow Howard-Snyder's rule about excluding evidence for the deity of Christ from outside the Trilemma itself. A person who looked at these four propositions in the light of the evidence for the resurrection set forth in a book like Morison's *Who Moved the Stone?*[59] and in the light of the fulfillment of prophecy, etc., might well come up with high enough values that the final result would still be quite believable. Howard-Snyder's "range" (.43-.77) is simply a recognition that people come to different conclusions. One who thought with good reason that the actual probability was .77 (or higher) would hardly be required to suspend judgment simply because people who think it is .43 exist. Still, whatever values we assign must be less than absolute certainty. So far, therefore, the diminishing probabilities argument at worst can only qualify our confidence in the conclusion of the Trilemma; it does not overturn it.

I think the analysis I just gave is correct; but I also think that there is a deeper problem with the probability argument. It is easy to forget that in the Trilemma we are not simply debating various abstract propositions but ultimately dealing with our response to a person. The purpose of the argument is to enable us more intelligently to answer the basic question Jesus puts to us: "Who do you say that I, the Son of Man, am?" (Matt 16.13–18).[60] Even Howard-Snyder admits that the Trilemma is deductively valid; his problem is the extent to which we can have confidence in the individual propositions.[61] But the bottom-line question is whether I trust this Person that the historical accounts and the preaching of the Gospel present to me—even when He makes

---

[59] Frank Morison, *Who Moved the Stone?* (Downers Grove, Il.: Inter Varsity Press, n.d).

[60] See Brazier, op. cit., 103–6.

[61] Howard-Snyder, op. cit., 457.

the most audacious claims. And one does not decide to trust another person simply by juggling a probabilistic calculus, but by responding to the gestalt of his total personality. Of course, one is justified in doing so only as long as the propositions of the formal argument are believable both individually and together. If they were not, the gestalt would not matter; if they were not, it would be a sign that the gestalt was leading you astray. But one does not decide to trust a person on the basis of propositions and their logical relationships alone.

In making this judgment in Jesus' case, we gain clarity by using the Trilemma: by asking, "Is He lying? Is He crazy? Could He be just simply mistaken about *this* claim?" The Christian hopes that the response will be, "In *His* case—no, I don't think so," and that the Trilemma will then help to guide the seeker toward the logical response of faith: "He is telling the truth." It will not be the Trilemma alone which generates this response, but rather the totality of Christ's person as revealed by the Gospel (aided and brought into focus by the Trilemma and its validity) and brought home to the seeker by the Holy Spirit. Nothing less has ever produced that response or ever will. I think Lewis understood this truth, for at the end of his presentation in *Mere Christianity* he hopes that his elimination of the great moral teacher copout will push us back to Christ himself: "*He* has not left that open to us. *He* did not intend to."[62]

The diminishing probability argument then is not as impressive as it first seems and is ultimately irrelevant to the way the Trilemma actually works.

A similar attempt to weaken the apparent force of the Trilemma is the "Extraordinary Claims" argument: According to

---

[62] Lewis, *Mere Christianity*, op. cit., 56, emphasis added.

this argument, an extraordinary claim (like the resurrection or deity of the man Jesus) requires extraordinary support. Historical arguments, by their nature never more than probabilistic, are inherently incapable of providing such support. Therefore, such claims cannot be supported by apologetic argument and must be believed if at all by sheer blind faith.

The problem with the argument from extraordinary claims is that it cuts both ways. Is the notion that this vast, intricate, mathematically rational and fine-tuned universe just randomly popped into existence out of nothing and then proceeded to organize itself by pure chance into DNA, etc., not an extraordinary claim? Is the notion that the Disciples were all transformed from clueless cowards to men who turned the world upside down by a contention they knew to be false not an extraordinary claim? Is the notion that a merely human person can believe himself to be the omnipotent, eternal Creator of the universe and not be insane not an extraordinary claim? Surely they are. So if, when you think it through, you can avoid one extraordinary claim only by affirming another set of them, equally extraordinary, we must realize that the argument from extraordinary claims takes us nowhere and should therefore be abandoned. We simply have to make the best judgment we can on the evidence we have, however "extraordinary" the conclusion may seem to some to be.

Application

How then do we evaluate the Trilemma as an apologetic argument? Brazier asks whether it is a failure and concludes, "No, because it generated speculation, got people talking."[63] It has certainly done at least that! And it has done much more as well.

---

[63] Brazier, op. cit., 186.

In conclusion, Lewis's Trilemma is still a strong argument and can be used with confidence if we allow it to be nuanced and strengthened by its context in Lewis's body of writings as a whole and if we understand its proper role in clarifying the options. It is unfair to take a paragraph aimed at a lay audience and complain that it is inadequate to deal with people who have a more sophisticated set of issues. Of course, the classic passage from *Mere Christianity* needs to be supplemented when used with more sophisticated audiences, by Lewis's other writings and by information and arguments that have come to light since he wrote. But the basic argument is sound. It is one thing to claim that it commits the fallacy of False Dilemma; it is quite another to show that other credible and valid options actually exist. As I have shown above, Lewis's critics have simply failed to do that.

The argument as presented by Lewis does not purport to prove the deity of Christ by itself, but it supports it by analyzing the logical options available and pointing out the difficulty of seeing Jesus as a liar or a lunatic. Attempts to add "Legend" to the Trilemma fail due to the demonstrable philosophical bias and methodological flaws of negative New-Testament scholarship. Attempts to see Jesus as a liar or a lunatic are tendentious and ignore the actual facts of his life. And attempts to find other options, such as a sane person sincerely mistaken about his deity, fail in the same way and fail doubly when we understand the real magnitude of the claim being made. Apologists who use the Trilemma today must be prepared to deal with the attempts to deflect it down one of those fruitless paths whenever they come up.

Moreover, Lewis's position as the dean of Christian apologists remains unchallenged. He was not infallible, but neither was he guilty of writing something in the Trilemma that was "not top-flight thinking."[64] His unique combination of wide learning, no-nonsense clarity, elegant language, and apt analogy remains as the standard to which we should all aspire and the example we should seek to emulate. When examined carefully, the Trilemma supports that conclusion; it is not an exception to it.

Liar, Lunatic, or Lord? Lacking, Ludicrous, or Logical? Plunk for Liar or Lunatic if you must. But let's not come with any patronizing nonsense about how Lewis gave us a fallacious argument. He has not left that open to us. He did not intend to.

---

[64] Hinten, "Approaches," op. cit., 8.

INTERLUDE

THE NOETIC EFFECTS OF SIN, II

Though Satan threatens always to deceive
    And oft the veil seems heavy on my face,
    Lord help mine unbelief, for I believe!
I've seen through every subtle wile he weaves
    And would with all my heart your truth embrace,
    But Satan threatens always to deceive.
The tyranny of sight gives no reprieve,
    More garish than the glimmers of your grace;
    Lord, help mine unbelief, for I believe.
The evidence is *there*; I do perceive
    It clearly and myself can make the case,
    But Satan threatens always to deceive.
The certainty you help me to achieve
    Can sometimes disappear without a trace;
    Lord, help mine unbelief, for I believe.
It's all so plain! How deeply you must grieve
    To see me still in doubting Thomas' place.
    Since Satan threatens always to deceive,
Lord, help mine unbelief, for I believe.

CHAPTER FIVE

"Made for Another World"
C. S. Lewis's Argument from Desire Revisited

Introduction

Though C.S. Lewis is perhaps better known for the Trilemma, The Moral Argument, and The Argument from Reason, his most characteristic argument may actually be The Argument from Desire. As one might expect, there have been varying views on how persuasive an argument it is. The recent *status quaestionis* discussion by Peter S. Williams and Gregory Bassham[1] gives us an excellent opportunity for a fresh look at that question.[2]

The Argument from Desire played an interesting supporting role in Lewis's own conversion that makes it unsurprising to find that it had a place in his apologetic. It was after all the experience of *sehnsucht*, or "joy," the intense longing aroused by inex-

---

[1] Gregory Bassham, ed., *C. S. Lewis's Christian Apologetics: Pro and Con* (Leiden: Rodopi, 2015), 27–74.

[2] Other recent treatments include, positively, Peter Kreeft, *Heaven: The Heart's Deepest Longing* (San Francisco, Ca: Ignatius Press, 1989; J. P. Moreland, *The God Question: An Invitation to a Life of Meaning* (Eugene, Or.: Harvest House, 2009), pp. 94–5; and Alister McGrath, *The Intellectual Life of C. S. Lewis* (Oxford: Wiley-Blackwell, 2014); and, negatively, John Beversluis, *C. S. Lewis and the Search for Rational Religion*, rev. ed. (Amherst, NY: Prometheus Books, 2007) and Erik Wielenberg, *God and the Reach of Reason* (NY: Cambridge Univ. Pr., 2008).

plicable beauty, that drove Lewis to his conversion in such a way that he calls it "the central story of my life."[3] He called "joy" "an unsatisfied desire which is itself more desirable than any other satisfaction."[4] He did not so much conclude directly from the experience of having this desire that God exists and that Jesus is His Son; rather, it was what kept him from being comfortable in Atheism until other arguments, such as Chesterton's and Tolkien's that Christ is the fulfillment of human mythology, led to his conversion.[5] His atheism was never able successfully to explain the fullness of his aesthetic and emotional life. As he wrote to Arthur Greeves while still in his atheist period,

> Faeries must be in the woods
> Or the satyr's merry broods,
> Tritons in the summer sea,
> Else how could the dead things be
> Half so lovely as they are? …
>
> Atoms dead could never thus
> Move the human heart of us,
> Unless the beauty that we see
> Part of endless beauty be.[6]

Joy or sweet desire kept Lewis from being comfortable as an atheist, but it did not in itself lead him to theism or to Christ. He tells us quite explicitly that his conversion was not the direct result of his unfulfilled desires: for all he knew, "the total rejection"

---

[3] C.S. Lewis, *Surprised by Joy: The Shape of my Early Life* (NY: Harcourt, Brace, and World, 1955), 17.

[4] Ibid., 17–18.

[5] Donald T. Williams, "G.K. Chesterton, *The Everlasting Man*," *C. S. Lewis's List: The Ten Books that Influenced Him Most*, ed. David Werther and Susan Werther. (NY: Bloomsbury, 2015), 34–6.

[6] C.S. Lewis, *The Collected Letters of C. S. Lewis*, 3 vols., ed. Walter Hooper (San Francisco, Ca: HarperSanFrancisco 2004), 1:373.

of what he called joy might have been "one of the demands" of his new faith.[7] Once he had come to faith, though, he went back and thought through the implications of his experience to be able to articulate more clearly how it functions as one of the "signposts" he had come to understand it to be by the end of his quest.[8] The fruit of that articulation is what we call the Argument from Desire. It is given in its simplest form in *Mere Christianity*:

The Argument

> Creatures are not born with desires unless satisfaction for those desires exists. A baby feels hunger: well, there is such a thing as food. A duckling wants to swim: well, there is such a thing as water. Men feel sexual desire: well, there is such a thing as sex. If I find in myself a desire which no experience in this world can satisfy, the most probable explanation is that I was made for another world.[9]

The argument does not need a lot of explanation. It starts with a proposition that is all but self-evident: The existence of a desire or a hunger implies the existence of something that could at least potentially fulfill it. Creatures do not want to eat unless they are designed to need food. So if human beings possess a hunger for spiritual fulfillment, there must be something extant that this hunger answers to. Given the universal existence of religions in human cultures, all trying to satisfy that hunger, we can assume that some spiritual reality exists—that, at a minimum, this world of temporal and empirical experience is not the only one that exists or that is relevant to our existence. (I think I

---

[7] Lewis, *Surprised by Joy*, op. cit., 230.

[8] Ibid., 238.

[9] C. S. Lewis, *Mere Christianity* (NY: MacMillan, 1960), 120.

just proved my point that the argument needs little explanation. You might well want to read Lewis's paragraph as the explanation of mine!)

Though Peter S. Williams and Gregory Bassham discuss several versions of the argument—deductive, inductive, abductive, *reductio*[10]—it is clear from Lewis's language that his version of the argument is not a deductive proof but an argument to the best explanation (i.e., abductive). *The Encyclopedia of Philosophy* defines abduction as "The type of reasoning that yields from a given set of facts an explanatory hypothesis for them."[11] That is an exact description of what Lewis attempted in the paragraph from *Mere Christianity* cited above. Lewis calls his conclusion "the most probable explanation" of the pattern in the phenomena of desire and fulfillment he had noted in babies, ducklings, and men. What needs explanation is the unexpected and anomalous occurrence of this one apparently unsatisfiable desire. It needs explanation because all other natural desires we encounter do seem to have appropriate objects.

Lewis was not the only person to have noticed this pattern. Philosopher of science Michael Polanyi wrote that "Our heuristic cravings imply, like our bodily appetites, the existence of something which has the properties required to satisfy us."[12] Why would this one craving be an exception? Lewis asks, in effect, what if it is not? Well, if it is not, then the Christian view of the next life makes sense.

---

[10] In Gregory Bassham, ed., *C. S. Lewis's Christian Apologetics: Pro and Con* (Leiden: Rodopi, 2015), 27–74.

[11] A. Boruch, "Logical Terms, Glossary of," *The Encyclopedia of Philosophy* (NY: MacMillan, 1967), 5:57.

[12] Michael Polanyi, *Personal Knowledge: Towards a Post-Critical Philosophy* (NY: Harper & Row, 1964), 129.

Critique

How could Lewis's argument be attacked? It assumes two states of affairs that could themselves be questioned. First, is the existence of a desire in fact evidence for the existence of the object of that desire? Lewis answers that being hungry doesn't prove you will be fed, but it does prove that you have a body that needs nourishment and that presumably therefore some kind of food exists. Therefore, the desire for Paradise does not prove that you are going to go there, but it does seem to indicate that such a thing exists.[13] I think Lewis's response so far is adequate, if in fact it can be established that people have a desire for paradise. And that leads to the other question.

Second, do people actually experience a real desire that no finite temporal thing can satisfy? Lewis thinks they do. Suppose your experience of desire is awakened by the beauty of the hillside you see in the distance. What will happen if you go there? "An easy experiment will show that by going to the far hillside you will get either nothing, or else a recurrence of the same desire which sent you thither."[14] Enough repetitions of this experiment might convince us that either the desire is an illusion or its fulfillment must be found elsewhere than in the finite world.

Yet many people deny that they experience any unsatisfiable desire. Either they think they have found satisfactions that are good enough, or they are confident that, if they just keep looking, they will do so. They may have repressed the desire, or they may still be trying to satisfy it with available objects: What is over the next hill, or the next woman, they tell themselves, will

---

[13] C. S. Lewis, "The Weight of Glory," *The Weight of Glory and Other Addresses*, ed. Walter Hooper (San Francisco, Ca: HarperCollins, 1980), 32–3.

[14] C. S. Lewis, *The Pilgrim's Regress: an Allegorical Apology for Christianity, Reason, and Romanticism* (Grand Rapids, Mi: Eerdmans, 1960), 9.

be what they are really looking for. They think the satisfaction is simply deferred. How do we know they are wrong? John Beversluis thinks they may not be: People may have the experience Lewis describes, but Beversluis thinks it is too nebulous to be accurately called a *desire*.

> The possibility of describing and accounting for such a state of mind as a *desire* in any minimally coherent sense depends on the person in that state of mind eventually discovering an object that not only *satisfies* her desire but which she also *recognizes* as the object she has been pursuing all along.[15]

Lewis would have had no problem with Beversluis's criterion; he would have said that he had satisfied it in finding Christ. Whether he had or not, is not a question a person outside that experience of encounter with Christ is in a position to evaluate. That is because the faith component in committing one's life to Christ cannot be eliminated: The argument from desire cannot be fully evaluated except experientially. Only when a person in honesty reckons with the fact that this final finding is just not going to happen in this world is he ready to consider the conclusion Lewis reached:

> If a man followed this desire, pursuing all the false objects until their falsity appeared and then resolutely abandoning them, he must come out at last into the clear knowledge that the human soul was made to enjoy some object that is never fully given—nay, cannot even be imagined as given—in our present mode of subjective and spatio-temporal experience.... And if nature makes nothing in vain, the One who can sit in this chair must exist.[16]

---

15 John Beversluis, *C. S. Lewis and the Search for Rational Religion* (Amherst, NY: Prometheus Books, 2007), 52.

16 Lewis, *Pilgrim's Regress*, op. cit., 10.

How strong is the Argument from Desire? Even if the initial dismissals and questionings of it above are rejected, it still has a couple of weaknesses. First, for people who deny having had the relevant experience, it is simply beside the point. It is possible that some of them may have had that experience and do not recognize it; others may be in denial about the impossibility of satisfying their deepest desires with temporal objects. But it would not be possible to prove that this is true of all of them; that would involve proving a negative. And even for those who have had the experience but deny it, the argument will have neither interest nor force. Even if the Argument from Desire is valid, it will tend to compel the attention only of people who have not only had, but who *recognize* themselves as having had, the relevant experience.

Second, as Bassham correctly points out, from the mere existence of unsatisfied desire it does not strictly follow that the object which supposedly exists for it is a god of any kind, much less the Christian God. One could equally spin the same facts to support the Buddhist notion that desire is the source of suffering and that therefore the wise course is to follow the Eightfold Path to its elimination. Bassham is right to point out that connecting the argument specifically to God as the postulated object "requires a further and perhaps more difficult argument... that Lewis does not provide."[17] At least, he does not provide it as part of the Argument from Desire itself. But surely Lewis could have responded that when the argument is made in *Mere Christianity* it is in a context that already has the Moral Argument and the Trilemma in the background; and that when they are combined, they do indeed point to Christ. The further arguments Bassham wants are ones that Lewis does in fact provide.

---

[17] Bassham, op cit., 51.

I would argue, then, that the Argument from Desire can contribute to a cumulative case for Christian theism in spite of these weaknesses, especially if we view it in the context of Lewis's other arguments. Lewis was too wise ever to claim that in itself it proves the existence of the Christian God. Recall his language: "most probable explanation"... "pretty good indication." But it does do what an abductive argument is supposed to do: It makes sense of a common human experience and points to the likely existence of *something* that is *compatible* with Christian theism and Christian fulfillment as expounded in the Bible and Christian theology, and which is very difficult to explain apart from that Christian account. Such desire is, in other words, one more aspect of human experience that makes perfectly good sense if Christianity is true and presents a very difficult problem if it is not.

For those who recognize in themselves the experience Lewis is describing, then, the Argument from Desire can help to turn that experience into a signpost, into, at the very least, one more reason to follow the arrow to see where the sign might be pointing. The argument from desire does not prove the existence of God by itself, but then it does not claim to. But it does help to confirm the many other arguments concerning the best explanation that point to the same conclusion—at least for some people. Even Bassham admits that the abductive form of the argument is the strongest and that it might offer "some confirming evidence for theism," but does not think this "anything to write home about."[18] I suppose it depends on whom one is writing to at home. There are certainly some people for whom that letter might be very significant indeed.

One conclusion might be that the argument from desire just doesn't work with a certain type of person. Perhaps some of us

[18] Ibid., 55

are just too emotionally undeveloped—or jaded—to be suscepti- ble. But I would suggest that we make a mistake by taking such people's statements denying transcendent desire at face value, certainly by accepting them as representative of the human race as a whole. Solomon tells us that "God has set eternity in their hearts" (Ecc 3.11).[19] If this is true, then the denial of transcendent desire is a smokescreen, a defense mechanism designed to protect atheists from reality—like the Narnian dwarfs of *The Last Battle* who insist that Aslan's country is a dirty stable and that violets are stable litter, too afraid of being taken in to be taken out of the prisons of their own limited thinking.[20]

Application

If Solomon was right, human beings are not in fact fully satis- fied by the temporal and physical, however hard they may try to convince themselves that they are. But one probably can't argue them out of their claim that they are. One can only try to arouse the desire, to fan it to the point where they cannot ignore it any- more. And the best way to do that might be to talk about the foretastes of fulfillment we have already been granted in Christ, or just to live a life of transcendent openness to Joy before them. If we can get them to read Thomas Traherne's *Five Centuries of Meditation*, it wouldn't hurt.

> Things unknown have a secret influence on the soul, and like the center of the earth unseen violently attract it. We love we know not what, and therefore everything allures us.... Do

---

[19] While the author's response to this declaration is ambiguous, its basic thrust is clear: As *The NIV Study Bible* glosses it, "God's beautiful but tantalizing world is too big for us, yet its satisfactions are too small. Since we were made for eternity, the things of time cannot fully and permanently satisfy." (Grand Rapids, MI: Zondervan, 1973): 1010.

[20] C. S. Lewis, *The Last Battle* (1956; NY: HarperTrophy, 1986), 185–6.

you not feel yourself drawn by the expectation of some Great Thing?... You never enjoy the world aright till you see how a [grain of] sand exhibiteth the wisdom and power of God.... You never enjoy the world aright till the sea itself floweth in your veins, till you are clothed with the heavens and crowned with the stars.... Infinite wants satisfied produce infinite joys.... You must want like a God that you may be satisfied like God. Were you not made in his image?[21]

Lewis learned the Argument from Desire from Augustine's Trinity-shaped vacuum and his heart that was "restless until it rests in Thee," as developed by Traherne, George Herbert, and George MacDonald. The argument will legitimately have a certain existential force for those in whose hearts Desire has been sufficiently aroused. The best service those earlier writers—and Lewis himself—can do us is perhaps just to fan that flame.

In us, let it burn.

---

[21] Thomas Traherne, *Centuries of Meditation*, in Alexander M Witherspoon. and Frank J. Warnke, *Seventeenth-Century Prose and Poetry*, 2nd ed. (NY: Harcourt Brace Jovanovich, 1982), 694, 696, 698.

INTERLUDE

SEHNSUCHT II

God knows no shame in what He will employ
   To win a wandering sinner back again.
   Thus, C.S. Lewis was surprised by joy.
A childish garden made to be a toy
   Of moss and twigs upon a biscuit tin?
   God knows no shame in what He will employ.
The silly garden helped him to enjoy
   The real ones, made him want to enter in.
   Thus, C.S. Lewis was surprised by joy.
Not Athens (first), Jerusalem, or Troy,
   But Squirrel Nutkin's granary and bin?
   God knows no shame in what He will employ.
When Balder the beautiful was dead, destroyed,
   The voice that cried it came into his ken;
   Thus, C.S. Lewis was surprised by joy.
But pagan legend! Could *that* be the ploy?
   Somewhere the path to Heaven must begin.
   God knows no shame in what He will employ;
Thus, C.S. Lewis was surprised by joy.

CHAPTER SIX

"Myth Become Fact"

C. S. Lewis and the Narrative Argument
for Christianity

Introduction

The Narrative Argument is not one of the traditional apologetic arguments, but it was an important one for Lewis. It was the argument which most directly led to his conversion when Tolkien convinced him on Addison's Walk that the Christian religion was true, not just because it is the antithesis of pagan mythology, but also because it is in some sense the fulfillment of pagan myth. How can this be? It seems problematic to many modern Christians who were raised to equate myth with untruth. If they can be patient enough to see how Lewis used that terminology, however, they might find some interesting insights that they could use.

Perhaps Lewis's most original contribution to the theology of revelation is the way he sees myth, including pagan myth, as a source of revelation—not of authoritative revelation (like Scripture) but of substantive revelation (like nature and history). This concept is "original," not in the sense that Lewis was the first to think of it (for he got the idea from Tolkien and from G.K. Chesterton before him), but because it is mainly through Lewis that most conservative Christians are first introduced to the idea that pagan myth could be anything other than false religion plain and simple. To understand Lewis's view here, we have to understand something about the peculiar way in which he returned from atheism and materialism to theism and then to Christian faith. Here is how it went down.

The Argument

As a young man Lewis had come to the place where he *cared for* nothing but the gods and heroes he had read about in pagan myths and yet *believed in* "nothing but atoms and evolution and military service."[1] The stab of "joy" or romantic longing (*sehnsucht*) that came to him through nature and the great myths seemed to hint at a larger world of meaning and purpose, but he thought there was no reason to believe in any of the religions that try to capture that meaning and purpose. He thought that modern knowledge had exploded them and left only materialism and cynicism in their place. But first G.K. Chesterton's book *The Everlasting Man* and then Christian friends like J.R.R. Tolkien began to challenge his pessimistic assumptions.

The first mention of *The Everlasting Man* in Lewis's autobiography gives it a significant role in preparing the young atheist for that fateful evening on Addison's Walk with J.R.R. Tolkien and Hugo Dyson in 1931 which would lead to Lewis's conversion:

> Then I read Chesterton's *Everlasting Man* and for the first time saw the whole Christian outline of history set out in a form that

---

[1] Lewis, *Surprised by Joy*, op. cit., 174.

seemed to me to make sense. Somehow I contrived not to be too badly shaken. You will remember that I already thought Chesterton the most sensible man alive "apart from his Christianity."[2]

How did *The Everlasting Man* prepare Lewis for the conversation with Tolkien and Dyson on Addison's Walk? The skeptical Lewis had that evening foolishly described myth and fairy tale as "lies breathed through silver," provoking from Tolkien the response that was later summarized in poetic form in the piece that became part of the essay "On Fairie Stories."

"Dear Sir," I said—"Although now long estranged
Man is not wholly lost or wholly changed.
Dis-graced he may be, yet is not dethroned,
And keeps the rags of lordship once he owned:
Man, Sub-creator, the refracted Light
Through whom is splintered from a single white
To many hues, and endlessly combined
In living shapes that move from mind to mind.
Though all the crannies of the world we filled
With Elves and Goblins, though we dared to build
Gods and their houses out of dark and light,
And sowed the seed of dragons—'twas our right
(Used or misused). That right has not decayed:
We make still by the law in which we're made.[3]

Tolkien's full response elaborated what he would later in that essay call the doctrine of sub-creation: Human beings are creative because we are created in the image of the Creator. We make (stories, among other things) because we are made in the image of the Maker whose creation is the Story we call the history of the uni-

[2] Ibid., 223
[3] J.R.R. Tolkien, "On Fairie Stories," *The Tolkien Reader* (NY: Ballantine, 1966): 54.

verse. A myth is one of those stories by which ancient people tried to explain the world. In other words, myth and its power as Lewis had experienced it can only fully be understood in the light of the Christian doctrine of the *imago Dei* (image of God), which explains what myth is, why it is, and why describing it simply as lies is just too simple. A myth is a story that tries to explain the world. Most of them are, of course, false considered literally, but the very attempt still moves a susceptible reader by showing him the potential for a significance that secularism cannot grasp. What if one such story were actually true, even literally and historically true? The other ones, even in their falsehood, might have prepared you for that astonishing realization by keeping the ideas of meaning and purpose before you and even hinting at what the real meaning and purpose of life might be. "Used or misused, that right has not decayed; / We make still by the law in which we're made."

Well, Lewis had already encountered in Chesterton the idea that Christianity is "that pure and original truth that was behind all mythologies like the sky behind the clouds."[4] In addition there was Chesterton's connection of "the philosophy of stories" with man's uniqueness: He is "a creator as well as a creature."[5] Thus, "Man is not merely an evolution but a revolution."[6] And this, as Chesterton explained, is why human stories, as reflections of The Human Story, are so unlike the apocryphal "history of cows in twelve volumes" with which he compares it, which "would not be very lively reading."[7]

So then, Tolkien and Dyson did not have to start from scratch. They were watering a seed that Chesterton had already planted

---

[4] G. K. Chesterton, *The Everlasting Man*, op. cit., 258.
[5] Ibid., 18.
[6] Ibid., 8.
[7] Ibid., 158. Cf. Williams, *Mere Humanity*, op. cit., 25–36.

when they told Lewis that, as he summarized the conversation later to his friend Arthur Greeves, "The story of Christ is simply a true myth: a myth working on us in the same way as the others, but with this tremendous difference that *it really happened.*" That explained why Lewis loved the great myths and fairy stories even without believing in them and why he loved the idea of sacrifice, especially a god sacrificing himself to himself, when he met it in other myths: They were adumbrations of the truth, "God expressing Himself through the minds of the poets, using such images as He found there, while Christianity is God expressing Himself through what we call 'real things.'"[8] And they were watering another Chestertonian seed when they told Lewis that the significance of myth flows from human nature as made in the image of the Maker. Both ideas were already there in *The Everlasting Man*, which had already shown Lewis the Christian outline of history in a way that made sense. And the connections between the two ideas were there too, waiting for Tolkien and Dyson at the right moment to pull them together.

The truth that lies behind all the great myths like the sky behind the clouds; the true myth that works on us like all the others but unlike them really happened: these ideas came together on Addison's Walk on September 19, 1931, and, as a result, on September 28 Lewis realized that he had finally come to believe that Christ was the Son of God while riding in Warnie's side-car on the way to the Whipsnade Zoo. It is easy to see then why, in the reading that led to Lewis's conversion, Chesterton ranks second only to MacDonald and no book ranks higher than *The*

[8] Lewis, *Collected Letters*, op. cit., 1:977; cf. Sayer, Jack, op. cit., 225–7 and Roger Lancelyn Green and Walter Hooper, *C. S. Lewis: A Biography* (NY: Harcourt Brace Jovanovich, 1974): 116–18.

Everlasting Man. It had "illuminated what Lewis already knew to be true and pulled all the previously disjointed pieces into a harmonious vision of reality."[9] It had prepared him to be able to understand and accept from Tolkien and Dyson the argument that was the tipping point in his journey to theism and Christian faith and that became central to his thinking from then on. (See for example the essay "Myth Became Fact," which is Lewis's way of saying the things he learned from Chesterton and Tolkien.[10]) For the rest of his life Lewis would recommend *The Everlasting Man* to anyone asking him for books along the same lines as his own popular expositions of and apologies for Christian faith.[11]

Critique

Lewis makes some conservative readers bristle when he talks about myth in Scripture, because most people who use that language use it to mean that the Bible is not essentially different from other ancient religious writings and that we can dismiss its historicity much more cavalierly than Lewis does. But if we understand how Lewis used that language, there is nothing inherently problematic about it, nothing inherently contradictory to historicity. Biblical myth is "myth become fact." "Just as God is none the less God by being Man, so the Myth remains Myth even when it becomes Fact. The story of Christ demands from us, and repays, not only a religious and historical, but also an imaginative

---

[9] Scott R. Burson & Jerry L Walls. *C. S. Lewis and Francis Schaeffer: Lessons for a New Century from the Most Influential Apologists of our Time* (Downers Grove, IL: IVP, 1998); 162.

[10] C. S. Lewis, "Myth Become Fact," *God in the Dock: Essays on Theology and Ethics*, ed. Walter Hooper (Grand Rapids, Mi: Eerdmans, 1970): 63–67.

[11] For more on Chesterton's influence on Lewis, see Donald T. Williams, "G.K. Chesterton, *The Everlasting Man*," *C. S. Lewis's List: The Ten Books that Influenced Him Most*, ed. David Werther and Susan Werther (NY: Bloomsbury, 2015): 31–48.

response[12]" This is a positive contribution to our appreciation of biblical revelation with some interesting apologetic applications. Yet there are some issues in Lewis's view of myth in Scripture.[13]

Lewis has a lot to say about the role of myth in Scripture in his brilliant book *Miracles*. There we have much intriguing insight but also many unanswered questions. The mythology of the Hebrews was "the mythology chosen by God to be the vehicle of the earliest sacred truths, the first step in that process which ends in the New Testament where truth has become completely historical."[14] The chosen mythology, chosen to give us the right picture of God, is a wonderful way of putting it. But this time the assumed religious evolution itself raises troubling questions. So Genesis, we presume, is pretty much simply myth? Myth has not *completely* become fact until we reach the New Testament? What does that say about the Exodus? Where do we draw the line, when Christ is presented as the Passover Lamb and the Lord's Supper is clearly a re-application of the Passover meal? It is all one seamless history to the biblical writers. "Just as, on the factual side, a long preparation culminates in God's becoming incarnate as Man, so, on the documentary side, the truth first appears in mythical form and then by a long process of condensing or focusing becomes incarnate as History."[15] Myth as Lewis understands it here is "at its best, a real though unfocused gleam of divine truth falling on human imagination."[16]

It is questionable then whether Lewis's view of myth's contribution to revelation is worked out in a way completely consistent with

---

[12] Lewis, *Miracles*, op. cit., 139.

[13] For a more detailed critique of those issues, see Williams, *Deeper Magic.*, op. cit., 63–65.

[14] *Miracles*, op. cit., 129.

[15] Ibid., 139.

[16] Ibid.

the full biblical doctrine of inspiration as regards its role in Scripture. His definition of myth—an unfocused gleam of divine truth falling on human imagination—works well for the classical myths. But in Scripture we need some better wrestling with the question of how far the work of the Holy Spirit in inspiration should be seen as having focused it. Fortunately, these problems do not compromise the way pagan myth functioned for Lewis as a preparation for Scripture once Chesterton and Tolkien had removed the stumbling blocks that had kept Lewis from seeing it as such.

What is the Narrative Argument then exactly? It is another abductive argument, that is, an argument to the best explanation. It identifies an aspect of human experience—the meaningfulness of story, particularly of myth—that is difficult to explain on a secular basis but which makes good sense if certain Christian doctrines are true. They answer the question Lewis was asking in the poem he wrote while still an atheist:

> Faeries must be in the woods
> Or the satyr's merry broods,
> Tritons in the summer sea,
> Else how could the dead things be
> Half so lovely as they are? ...
>
> Atoms dead could never thus
> Move the human heart of us,
> Unless the beauty that we see
> Part of endless beauty be.[17]

The question functions in a parallel way to its role in the Argument from Desire (see chapter 5). There, if evolution has been adapting me to function in a purely material world, and if that is

---

[17] Lewis, *Collected Letters*, op. cit., 1:173.

the totality of my existence, then why do I have desires for things not in this world? That only makes sense if this world is not the only world. Here, if I am just a collection of atoms thrown together by evolution, why do I respond so deeply to story arcs that are about anything other than the survival of the fittest? The myth of Orpheus and Eurydice, for example, is not about the survival of anyone. Eurydice is lost more crushingly as a result of Orpheus's quest than she was by mere death. Their story rubs our noses in the question of how that aching emptiness can possibly have a meaning. It does not exactly answer that question, but it won't let us ignore it. What is the survival value (if evolution is supposed to be our ultimate story) of the hunger for meaning that such stories feed? Are the people with that hunger best described as chance collections of atoms or as makers made in the image of the Maker whose creation unfolds as a plot with the definite arc of creation, fall, and redemption? Again, those people only make sense if the world of atoms in motion is not the only world.

The existence of stories and of myths, the most meaning-intensive stories, does not of itself prove that God exists or that Jesus is His Son. But they are pointers to these realities when they are seen in the right context. They were for Lewis and Tolkien, and they can be for us.[18]

Application

The biggest change since Lewis wrote that is relevant to the Narrative Argument is the rise of Post-Modern "theory" with its radical rejection of the very possibility of knowing objective

---

[18] For an excellent discussion of myth and its significance in Lewis, see Charlie W. Starr, *The Faun's Bookshelf: C. S. Lewis on Why Myth Matters* (Kent, OH: Black Squirrel Books, 2018). For further discussion see also Williams, *Mere Humanity*, op. cit., 55–64.

truth. Specifically, we will now meet people for whom "narrative" is conceived, not as a potential path to truth, but as a substitute for truth. Given the alleged impossibility of any viewpoint that is not determined by one's race, class, gender, or historical "situatedness," all that is left is our personal "narrative," the way we choose to tell our story. We all have a narrative, but what we must not do is "privilege" one of them as *the* story, that is, the true Story. Post-Modernists think it inconceivable that there could be a foundational Story (with a capital S) that is objectively true, true for everyone whether they see or accept it or not, and into which our individual stories (lower-case s) must therefore fit if they are to be true and helpful narratives that point to real meaning rather than meaning that is only arbitrary and personal. In other words, there can be no valid "metanarrative." The mere suggestion that there could be such a Story is rejected out of hand as not only deluded but evil—it can only be a means of "imposing" one's values on others. And that is the ultimate evil.

People influenced by this particular version of perspectivalism may rightly see that narrative is a way we create meaning for ourselves. This insight might predispose them to discern the significance of the Narrative Argument. Unfortunately, in their case it comes with a set of assumptions that undermine that significance. If we are not careful, we may unintentionally find ourselves presenting a Christ who is not the way, the truth and the life, but only a way, a truth, and a life—because that is all our audience is capable of conceiving. If our hearers understand the exclusiveness of the claims of Christ, they may think it a *prima facie* reason to reject them. If they do not, whether because we have soft-pedaled them in fear of that rejection or because they have heard our message through the lens of their assumptions, they will be confronted with a very different Jesus from one who strides through the pages of the Gospels.

But this is a false Christ, the son of a lesser god. A Christ who is only lord of my perspectives is not the Lord of reality, and hence he is not capable of saving anybody. We must therefore resist the temptation to think we have to compromise the objectivity of the Christian truth claims in order to win any audience at all. It does no good to gain an audience only by losing our message. How then can we help Post-Modern people get past this huge stumbling block? Here are four suggestions.

First, while we are careful not to compromise on the issue of objective truth, we must be equally careful to approach that issue with the real humility that is perceived to be incompatible with our claim to have objective truth. We must truly see ourselves as beggars telling other beggars where we found bread—epistemological bread as well as soteriological bread, the bread of truth as much as the bread of salvation. Merely by virtue of talking about real truth, we will be heard as people who think they are so brilliant that they have figured out what is an inaccessible mystery to the entire rest of humanity. That is the default setting we will confront—unless we are intelligently proactive in counteracting it. This humility cannot be a front we put on; it must be real heart attitude we have cultivated by dying to self. It must be ground into us that we have truth on the same basis that we have forgiveness: only by the grace, the unmerited favor, of the God who stoops to us in revelation as He does in redemption. This humility cannot be faked. There is no substitute for dying to self if we are to have credibility, much less success. I urge you at this point to revisit theses four and five from the Introduction to this book on the spiritual preparation of the Apologist.

How do we show this humility once we have it? Its presence or absence will be perceived whatever we do, but we can help people notice it by following the second suggestion: Become adept at using Socratic Questions. You are asking the other person's opinion, not just trumpeting your own view. Then you can respond, "Well, that is very interesting. But have you considered....?" Who can object to that? If done skillfully, such questions can plant ideas that would not be entertained if they were presented head on. But a warning: They must be a real expression of humility before the Truth. They will backfire in a heartbeat if they are asked in a "Gotcha!" spirit. How many times have I seen people do more harm than good by skipping straight to this second suggestion without having stopped by the first!

Third, use those Socratic Questions to point out the contradictions inherent in Post-Modern perspectivalism. "So, this skepticism about all metanarratives: Would that not be a... metanarrative?" Hmmm. Surely most metanarratives are false, but what if there were one that wasn't? How might we tell? Every math problem has an infinite number of wrong answers, so we can see what you mean about being skeptical about metanarratives. But does their very wrongness not imply the existence of one (and only one) right answer? Can you *know* in advance that this one is impossible to find? (If your conversation partner says no, then the possibility of truth has been established. If the answer is yes, it leads to the follow-up question: If you can know *that*, what else might we be able to know?) Hmmm. We must become skeptical about our skepticism to make room for truth to be received.

Fourth, present the positive benefits of being able to know some important objective truths. You can be confident that people reject that possibility because they think it enhances their freedom to believe whatever they find meaningful and do whatever they desire. You can also be confident that there is a hunger for real truth and real meaning hiding beneath the surface waiting to be awakened. You fear objective truth, we can tell them, because you understand that if it existed and someone had it, it would confer great power—and you don't trust conservative Christians with that kind of power over your life. "I don't blame you," we can add. "I don't either." But what if there were one Person who *could* be trusted with that kind of power? What if that precise power would let him give us life, and that more abundantly? Could Jesus be that Person? Hmmm.

C.S. Lewis showed us the way. In defending the concept of truth against the forms of relativism that already existed in his day, he anticipated the more virulent forms that were coming. If by "New York" each of two men meant only the city he was imagining in his own head, if there were no actual New York to which those two images could be compared, we could not speak of truth or falsehood at all.[19] For Lewis the stubborn persistence of the actual New York in existence is a touchstone that allows the comparison to be fruitful by limiting how far perspectives can be self-authenticating just by existing. He understood that we have to answer the question "What is truth" before we can answer the question "What is true?"[20] And he showed us that, once

[19] Lewis, *Mere Christianity*, op. cit., 25.

[20] For a discussion of Lewis's defense of the correspondence theory of truth and its significance, see Williams, *Deeper Magic*, op. cit., 26–49. Cf. also Douglas Groothuis, *Truth Decay: Defending Christianity against the Challenges of Postmodernism* (Downers Grove, IL: InterVarsity Press, 2000).

we have cleared away the misconception that differing narratives about truth are all we can have, we can see the biblical Story of Creation, Fall, Redemption, and Restoration as our Story, and in it find meaning and truth that bring life indeed.

INTERLUDE

COMMENTARY, 1 PETER 3.15

We are to keep ourselves in readiness
    Should any ask a reason for the hope
    That is within us and which we confess.
The great Deceiver does not sleep or rest,
    Enticing people toward the slippery slope,
    And so we keep ourselves in readiness.
The Truth is lovely in a silken dress;
    Her servant comes in sackcloth tied with rope,
    A humble penitent who must confess
His great unworthiness, but also stress
    Her grace, the only reason he can cope,
    And thus he keeps himself in readiness.
We are but beggars sharing our success
    With other tramps who also want to grope
    Toward the light with us. And we confess
That ours is not the brilliance we express.
    Christ is the Light; we aim the telescope:
    That's how we keep ourselves in readiness
To justify the great Hope we confess.

CHAPTER SEVEN

God's Megaphone
C. S. Lewis and the Problem of Evil

Introduction

Apologetics has two phases. In positive apologetics, we make the positive case for Christianity, giving reasons why we should believe the Christian faith to be true. In negative apologetics, we defend the faith against the case from the other side, from reasons that have been advanced purporting to show why we should not believe it to be true. The chapters above focus on Lewis's positive apologetic, though certain negative arguments (e.g., skeptical biblical criticism) had to be dealt with in the process as they came up. Here we will look at his major foray into negative apologetics. He chose to mount his defense against the argument that Christians and skeptics agree is the biggest gun in the atheist arsenal: the problem of evil or of pain.[1] In its simplest form, the argument goes like this:

1. If God were good, He would want to eliminate evil.
2. If God were omnipotent, He would be able to eliminate evil.

---

[1] Lewis deals with this issue primarily in his first apologetic book, *The Problem of Pain* (1940; NY: MacMillan, 1967). For my own take on the question, see *The Young Christian's Survival Guide*, op. cit., 114–121.

3. But evil exists.

4. Therefore, God is either not good or not omnipotent (or does not exist). In either case, the Christian concept of God as a Being who exists as both good and omnipotent is alleged to have been shown to be incoherent and not believable.

The Argument from Evil is a strong argument for two reasons. First, it appears to be logical and cogent. It is formally valid: Given the premises, the conclusion follows. Then, each premise is something that orthodox Christians are required to accept. You cannot deny God's goodness, His omnipotence, or the existence of evil and be faithful to Scripture or to the Christian tradition in any of its manifestations. Therefore, the conclusion seems to follow logically from those premises. It would seem on the surface that of the three propositions, God's goodness, His omnipotence, and the existence of evil, that any two could be true without contradiction but not all three.

Second, the argument has emotional overtones that can easily cloud the judgment. It does not pose a purely academic philosophical challenge but rather a gut-wrenching existential one. People who have been badly hurt, or whose loved ones have been badly hurt, wonder why a good God could permit this to happen. They are not just skeptical about God; they are angry with God, and this anger sears the apparent logic of the argument deeply into their consciousness.

The argument's apparent logical cogency and its actual emotional impact, combined with the fact that it necessarily deals with matters such as the freedom of the will that are inherently mysterious in their own right, make it a tough apologetic hill to climb. (Theodicy is the branch of theology and apologetics that tries to climb it.) Lewis is fully aware of these difficulties, and so begins by noting his amateur status and limiting himself to the intellectual aspects of the question, wisely noting that "When pain is to be borne, a little courage helps more than much knowledge, a little human sympathy more than much courage, and the least tincture of the love of God more than all."[2] He then turns his attention to what his little book can do to clarify the intellectual issues.

The Argument

I have already hinted that the Argument from Evil is less conclusive than it initially appears to be. Lewis ranges over vast tracts of theology, philosophy, and psychology in the process of addressing it, but I will focus on three ways in which he dismantles that appearance of cogency. First, he steps back to ask, "Where did we ever get this idea of a God who is simultaneously absolutely good and absolutely powerful in the first place?" There might be reasons for it that are just as strong as the apparent reasons against it in the critique. Second, realizing that we cannot attack the argument's formal validity nor attack its premises directly, Lewis attacks the premises indirectly by showing that they gain their force by assuming definitions of key terms such as goodness and omnipotence that are not in fact the ones actually held by informed Christians. If he is successful, then the formal validity of the argument is fatal only to the definitions of divine goodness and omnipotence that it assumes, not to those actually held by Christians. Finally, having established in the first two steps the logical *possibility* that the existence of evil might be compatible with the existence of a good and omnipotent God, Lewis tries to

---

[2] *Problem of Pain*, op. cit., viii.

show a plausible rationale for where evil came from and how it might function in the plan of a good God.

Lewis begins with an unexpected move that casts the whole question in a new light. He notices that the very strength of the case against God from the existence of evil proves to be its Achilles' heel. That very strength in other words begs a question that is not often asked: If the world is so full of suffering as in fact it is, what ever made us think of it as the creation of a good and wise God? That conclusion is surely not a simple deduction from our experience of life.

To answer that question requires an understanding of the history of religion. It begins with the experience of "the numinous": a sense of fear and awe aroused by supernature or by nature as it hints to us of supernature independently of their ability to harm us. You fear a lion's teeth, but why do you fear a ghost? Not exactly because of anything you think it is going to *do* to you, says Lewis. Lewis, writing to Westerners, assumed perhaps a little too quickly that his readers will not be concerned about physical harm from the ghost. But even if you are an animist who fears that the ghost might curse you, *this* fear (numinous awe) transcends your fear of the specific provisions of that curse. And that part of the fear (numinous awe) would persist even if you believed the numinous being to be wholly benevolent. The experience Lewis is talking about is the fear that is left over after any fear of physical harm has been eliminated from consideration. It is perhaps best captured by the passage Lewis cites from *The Wind in the Willows* where Rat and Mole meet the god Pan: Mole asks Rat if he is afraid. "Afraid? Of him? O, never, never!" is Rat's response. "And yet, O Mole, I am afraid."[3]

---

[3] Ibid., 6.

The second element common to all religions is morality—like numinous awe, a response to our experience of life that that seems to be demanded by it but cannot be simply deduced from that experience. As we saw in the Moral Argument, "You can shuffle 'I want,' and 'I am forced,' and 'I shall be well advised,' and 'I dare not' as long as you please without getting out of them the slightest hint of 'ought' and 'ought not.'"[4] Yet there the "ought" is, and it cannot be avoided. In primitive religions, the numinous and the moral are not necessarily connected. (Think of the hardly chaste amorous adventures of the Greek gods.) A big jump comes when the Hebrews identify the numinous God of the Burning Bush and Sinai as the Source of the moral law. The last step is the historical event of the coming of Christ, whose life, death, and resurrection convinced His followers that He was that very Old-Testament God incarnate in space and time for their redemption.[5]

The upshot of this discussion is the realization that people did not naturally believe in a good Creator only to have this comforting philosophical position challenged by their experience of evil. "Christianity is not the conclusion to a philosophical debate on the origins of the universe; it is a catastrophic historical event following on the long spiritual preparation of humanity." In other words, Christianity "is not a system into which we have to fit the awkward fact of pain; it is itself one of the awkward facts which have to be fitted into any system we make."[6] If Christianity is true, then the intervention of God into the history of the world in the Exodus and in Christ gives us reasons for believing in a good God that are quire independent of our experiences of evil, reasons

[4] Ibid., 8.
[5] Ibid., 11–13.
[6] Ibid., 12.

that do not depend on our analysis of the relative amounts of pleasure and suffering in human experience. There would be no *problem* of evil if God had not given us reasons to believe in Him. There would just be evil. But that would be a different philosophical problem, equally difficult to solve: On what grounds could we then call suffering or any other misfortune *evil*?

Lewis starts then by leveling the playing field. He shows that it is not only Christians who face philosophical difficulties with their view of evil. Atheists simply have a different but at least equally intractable problem: how to justify thinking of evil as evil. On their view, it can be nothing more than aspects of the universe they do not happen to like. But surely that is an inadequate view and one that nobody actually holds, as you can show by attempting to steal the wallet of the person who claims to hold it. (See our discussion of the Moral Argument in chapter one above.)

Lewis then turns to the terms of the Argument from Evil itself. Let us recall its structure:

1. If God were good, He would want to eliminate evil.
2. If God were omnipotent, He would be able to eliminate evil.
3. But evil exists.
4. Therefore, God is either not good or not omnipotent (or does not exist).

The argument is formally valid. That is, if the premises are true, the conclusion must infallibly follow from them. And the premises are all statements to which Christian orthodoxy is committed, so we cannot avoid the conclusion by simply denying one of the premises. The two major ways of attacking an argument—showing that it is invalid or that one of its premises is factually incorrect—are off the table. But when this is the case and the conclusion still seems wrong, there is still one move left: We can examine the key terms and question their definitions. The premises might not be true in the way the argument needs them to be in order to reach its conclusion. Lewis therefore examines two key terms: omnipotence and goodness. It turns out that the argument uses them so loosely that it loses its ability to make a serious critique of specifically Christian doctrine.

The argument works, for example, only of we take omnipotence to mean that God can do anything. But omnipotence does not mean that at all. It literally means "all powerful": God's power is not limited. He can do anything that is "intrinsically possible," that is, anything that does not involve a logical contradiction. For example, God cannot make a square circle any more than you or I could, because if He makes it round it will not have four corners, and if He gives it four ninety-degree angles it will not be round. More power will not help if you are trying to do this nonthing. But it is not that God is frustrated in His attempt to do it. It is not in the nature of a square circle to be drawn because it is not in God's nature to try to draw it. Because God is the source of logic, the law of non-contradiction is part of His character. The fact that He is a God of truth and covenant faithfulness, in other words, is the reason why the law of non-contradiction holds in every possible world. As Lewis brilliantly summarizes it, "Meaningless combinations of words" (like "square circle") "do not suddenly acquire meaning just because we prefix to them the two other words 'God can.'"[7]

It follows that God's omnipotence does not enable Him to do a number of things that would seem to be required if He were to make a world containing free creatures and yet also containing no

[7] Ibid., 16.

possibility of evil. He cannot grant freedom and not grant it. He cannot grant free will and have there be no consequences to the way it is used. In other words, God could make a world containing no evil, but it could not contain *us*: not-yet-fully-redeemed fallen creatures. To ask Him to have done so is to ask for a square circle. Why then did He create such a complex and problematic thing as what we have turned out to be? Because a world of automata, of robots perfectly programmed rather than free creatures, would not have been worth making. People who imagine a world without evil always imagine it containing themselves as free creatures—which is, again, a square circle.

The second term that Lewis unpacks is goodness. First, God's goodness is higher than our concept of goodness, but not sheerly different from it. If it were sheerly different, we would not be able to talk of good and evil at all. God's goodness differs from our concept not as white differs from black but in the way a perfect circle differs from a child's first attempt to draw a circle.[8] We might not even as adults be able to draw a perfect circle freehand, but we can tell when we are getting closer.

People who find God's goodness incompatible with the existence of evil tend to reduce goodness to kindness. God's goodness, of course, includes kindness or benevolence, but there is a lot more to it than that. It includes justice, for example. And it includes a rigorous and uncompromising love. Love does not just want to see its object happy, with no regard to the effect of that happiness on its character. As Lewis puts it, he would not think much of the love of a friend who "cared only for my happiness and did not object to my becoming dishonest."[9] So the existence

---

[8] Ibid., 27.
[9] Ibid., 37.

of suffering is incompatible with the existence of a loving God only if we "attach a trivial meaning to the word 'love.'"[10] Again we notice that Lewis is not discussing the existence of evil in the abstract, but rather the existence of evil *in this world*: a world containing free creatures (specifically us) who have fallen but who are, some of them at least, being redeemed. So the concept of freedom, or perhaps better the capacity for significant choice, is central to his defense.

So far Lewis has reframed the question by showing that (1) there are reasons for believing in a good God that are just as strong as any challenge presented to that belief by the Argument from Evil and (2) that those who reject God on the basis of that argument simply trade one problem for another. Then he has showed that if we replace the simplistic notions of omnipotence and goodness in the premises of the argument with the more sophisticated conceptions of those ideas actually held by informed Christians, those premises no longer necessarily render the existence of evil incompatible with the existence of the Christian God. This is especially seen when that simple picture is filled out by what has been called the Free-Will Defense: The existence of free creatures is the greater good that justifies the temporary toleration of evil. Now it remains to suggest a plausible scenario for the origin of evil.

Lewis assumes that something like the biblical Fall lies in humanity's past. His plausible scenario or "likely tale"[11] is about how it happened. The speculative element concerns only the mode, not the fact, of the Fall. He imagines that God used evolution to create the bodies of the first human beings and then supernaturally

---

[10] Ibid., 36.
[11] Ibid., 64.

caused a spiritual nature and self-consciousness to "descend" upon them. At some point, they decided that they wanted to "call their souls their own," to live independently of God. But that meant to live a lie—to be "as God" rather than to live as a creature. "This act of self-will on the part of the creature, which constitutes an utter falseness to its true creaturely position" is the sin that constituted the Fall.[12] It might have involved eating a literal forbidden fruit. But the lie at the heart of it was its essence, and the attempt to live that lie inevitably corrupted both mankind's nature and its relationship to the Nature that was its environment. And this was the breach that let the experience of evil and suffering into the natural world, considered as man's world.

These considerations do not, of course, of themselves prove that the Christian account of God, good, and evil are true. What Lewis intends them to do here is all that can be legitimately asked of them: to show that, if we do have reasons for thinking Christianity to be true, the Argument from Evil fails to disprove them.

Critique

How well does Lewis's defense of Christian faith against the Argument from Evil succeed? It is important to remember the purpose of such a defense. The full case for why we should think Christianity is true must be made elsewhere. All that is required here is that the claim of the negative argument to overturn that case be defeated. Tallon notes correctly that "If [Lewis's] challenge to either premise succeeds, then the argument fails to refute traditional Christian theism."[13] Lewis does not give a complete

[12] Ibid., 68.
[13] Philip Tallon, "Pro: *The Problem of Pain* Defended," *C. S. Lewis's Christian Apologetics: Pro .and Con*, ed. Gregory Bassham (Leiden" Brill/Rodopi, 2015): 213.

answer to every question we have about the problem of evil because such an answer is not possible. Because the Argument from Evil purports to show that simultaneous belief in God and in evil is logically impossible—that affirming divine omnipotence, divine goodness, and existent evil involves a contradiction—any hole we can poke in it leaves Christian theism still standing if there are legitimate reasons elsewhere for believing in it (as we tried to show in the earlier chapters where Lewis makes his positive case). And Lewis's critique of the simplistic definitions implied in the initial premises shows that, when aimed at the *specifically Christian* account of God, good, and evil, the argument simply misses its target.

Despite its general success, some conservative Christians themselves will have issues with Lewis's presentation here. Many will think he concedes far too much to naturalistic evolution in his account of human origins. That is a legitimate discussion for another time and place. Here, it is sufficient to note that the *fact* of the Fall and its *nature* as rebellion against God are the points required for the defeat of the argument. On those points Lewis offers no compromise. And his analysis of its involving a lie about our creaturehood is both biblical and insightful. We do not need to agree with him on every point to recognize the usefulness of the positive contributions Lewis makes to our understanding of these issues.

Another potential issue for some is Lewis's dependence on the Free-Will Defense. Free will is a phenomenon notoriously difficult to define which is itself a bone of contention in Christian theology. But in the context of this discussion, that should not be a problem. Calvinists and Arminians disagree about the extent to which human freedom was compromised by the Fall. But they should agree that human beings were intended to be, were created to be, and are being restored in redemption to being creatures who, via their creation in the image of God, have the capacity for significant choice. If they had that status before the Fall and are being restored to it by salvation, that is sufficient to establish the greater good for the sake of which evil could theoretically be justified. Our intramural theological debates can therefore continue in another room without needing to interfere with our apologetic on this topic.

Lewis's critics seem to me to be particularly weak in this area. Beversluis thinks Lewis's definitions of key terms are arbitrary special pleading: He "ascribes new meanings to them that are not only absent from ordinary usage but often at variance with it."[14] The ignorance of the history of the use of those terms and their discussion in Christian theology that lies behind that claim is astonishing. Lewis simply distinguishes their actual meaning in standard Christian teaching about the attributes of God from popular usage. If someone is trying to refute the Christian understanding of these matters, surely that is the only proper way to proceed in countering that attempted refutation.

Beversluis's rebuttal of Lewis's conclusion that a good God could very well have a legitimate use for suffering in our lives is simply to restate his rejection of that conclusion by repainting it in the most unflattering terms possible. God's jealousy makes Him "a monumentally petty and self-absorbed deity."[15] "An allegedly good God who *uses* people—to the point of inflicting pain on innocent children—in order to achieve his own ends bespeaks a

---

[14] Beversluis 2007, op. cit., 229.
[15] Ibid., 251.

theology that is not only morally repugnant but barbaric."[16] "Any deity whose "plan" requires the violation of human rights and the infliction of suffering on the innocent... would be well advised to rethink his "plan.""[17] But this is not a refutation of Lewis's case or anyone's case that a good God could have legitimate reasons for creating a world that includes evil. It is simply a reframing of the issue by a person who refuses to consider the possibility that God could be *God*. It treats God the way we would legitimately treat Him if he were simply another human being, our equal. But human beings have "rights" only *under* God, with respect to each other. It has been held as self-evident that they are endowed by the Creator. Beversluis then is simply refusing to address the real problem as it is properly stated. He trusts his strong language to obscure the fact that he is not actually dealing with the questions of whether *God* could allow evil at all.

David L. O'Hara, in responding to Philip Tallon's defense of Lewis's argument in Gregory Bassham's "pro and con" book on Lewis's apologetic, cannot find anything exactly "wrong" in either Lewis or Tallon. He is reduced to claiming that Lewis's argument is of "limited value" because it might seem stronger than it really is, because it potentially leads to bad pastoral theology, and because it depends too much on speculation.[18] The first two objections are rather speculative themselves, in that they are about how people *might* respond. But does Lewis really set them up to respond in those ways? His humility comes through from the admission of amateur status in the first pages and could be taken as example-setting. Job's friends we have always with us, and

---

[16] Ibid.

[17] Ibid.

[18] Davd. L. O'Hara, "Con: C.S. Lewis on Evil: At Best a Likely Story," *C. S. Lewis's Apologetics: Pro and Con*, ed. Gregory Bassham (Leiden: Brill/Rodopi, 2015): 227–36.

they can probably find ammunition anywhere, including here. But Lewis is explicit that he is only dealing with the intellectual aspects of the problem. Pastoral application is an important topic, but it is beyond the scope of Lewis's book. Finally, it is hard to avoid the speculative element. I cannot see how it is a problem as long as one does not try to hide it. After all, the purpose of the book (and the need of the argument) is not to explain in detail how every concrete historical example of suffering is justified (an impossible task), but to show that plausible scenarios exist in which that justification could obtain.

In sum, Lewis's theodicy in *The Problem of Pain* does what we can reasonably expect a theodicy to do: It does not fully explain the mystery of evil, but it makes it possible to have faith in a good God even in the light of that mystery if there are compelling reasons outside the discussion of evil *per se* to do so. And as those reasons include the life, character, death, and resurrection of Jesus Christ, they remain compelling indeed.

Application

In the years since Lewis wrote, there has come about a decreased presumption of God's goodness on the part of the general public, a greater readiness to stand in moral judgment over Him (or over those horrible Christians' ideas about him) than Lewis had to face. It is therefore more important than ever that we be prepared to show that the goodness of God makes sense. O'Hara commits a false dilemma when he says that people need love and compassion rather than a theology in which God makes sense.[19] They truly need both. But they usually do need to experience love and compassion before they are ready to hear an explanation

---

[19] Ibid., 227.

of them. This has been true from of old, but it is even more important that we remember it today. From the fact that the book Lewis was invited to write deals with the explanation, it does not follow that he would have disagreed with this analysis or failed to supply the compassion.

The argument itself has seen a few permutations since Lewis wrote. An important one is the introduction of the concept of "gratuitous evil." "Okay," the current skeptic might respond, "maybe people like Lewis have shown that it is *theoretically* possible that evil could be justified by a higher good. But does it have to be *this much* evil?" Then an example will be forthcoming of some evil for which it is hard to find any conceivable compensatory greater good that the particular evil *had* to exist to support: a baby deer painfully burned to death in a forest fire, a horrible cancer ravaging a child, the sexual abuse of a child. That is gratuitous evil—evil that serves no conceivable higher purpose.

Lewis does not address the issue of gratuitous evil directly, but we had better be prepared to do so today. In that response it is important to resist the temptation to try to find an explanation for the examples of gratuitous evil that are offered. There is a reason why you risk sounding lame and doing more harm than good if you try. We simply do not have the kind of exhaustive view of the web of cause and effect that would be required to know the explanation in most cases. But this inability cuts both ways. If it would take omniscience to know with any assurance what is *not* a case of gratuitous evil, if would also take it to know what *is* in fact such a case. But while this realization is part of the answer, it is not a sufficient answer in itself. Why not? There are surely many events in our experience that are going to look like gratuitous evil to people who will feel that the burden of proof is on us that they are not. There is a mystery of evil that is left after all the explaining we can do.

How do we move past this impasse? If we must accept the goodness of God by faith in the light of strong apparently contrary evidence, what could justify such faith? That is really the challenge we face. That is really the proper way to ask the question. That is the question we must be able to answer. Lewis provides the key to answering it in what may be the strongest part of his case in *The Problem of Pain*: his reframing of the question at the outset. A version of the question that we need to keep on the table is why anybody ever thought a good God could be behind this world in the first place. And here we must remember Lewis's point that Christianity is not the answer to a philosophical problem but the response to a catastrophic event.

Christians, in other words, do not believe that God is good because they have done the math. They do not believe that God is good because they have calculated that precisely X amount of suffering, considered in terms of distribution times intensity, would be the threshold where evil becomes gratuitous, but the world actually contains only X minus one. They believe that God is good because Jesus died for their sins. And they believe that this sacrifice is truly the demonstration of God's goodness because God raised Him from the dead. If Christians are right about that, then they are right about evil. If they are not, then they are of all men most miserable, as the Apostle Paul saw long ago.

In the absence of any calculus by which either believers or skeptics could credibly determine the boundary conditions of the gratuitous, then, the only place where the question of gratuitous evil can be profitably discussed is at the foot of the Cross. As with every apologetic argument, at the end of it we should try to lead people there.

How do the questions finally shake out in that place? They look like this. Why should we trust in the goodness of God despite the existence of apparently gratuitous evil, despite our inability to explain every example of it? Because if we don't, we will be left with the problem of how even to call it evil. Because Jesus died for our sins. Because God raised Him from the dead. Because the historical evidence for His crucifixion and resurrection is powerfully strong. Because the full combination of these considerations gives us a strong justification for exercising precisely that faith in precisely those terms. Because, exercising that faith, we have discovered that the only place where the universe makes sense is the spot where the shadow of the Cross falls across the mouth of the Empty Tomb.[20] And because C.S. Lewis helps to point us to this place in the ways we have seen above.

Thanks be to God.

---

[20] See Williams, *The Young Person's Survival Guide*, op. cit., 114–121, for further discussion of the problem of evil in these terms, and 11–19 for further discussion of the evidence for the resurrection of Christ.

INTERLUDE

THEODICY

Hopkins knew the Lord was just, yet pled
    The justice of his own request for rain.
    The Psalmist's echoed accents make it plain,
It wasn't the first time such words were said.
Even Jesus wondered as he bled
    Why God had turned His back upon the pain.
    The Spirit's calculus of loss and gain
Cannot be quickly figured in your head.

So when like Job we groan and question why
    And plead our case, but seem to plead in vain,
We might remember that the Lord's reply
    Was simply a refusal to explain,
And then a pure, white Lamb who lived to die.
    It is enough: We follow in His train.

CHAPTER EIGHT

An Answer for Orual
Lewis as Practical Role Model for Effective Apologists

"You are yourself the answer. Before your face questions die away."[1]

Introduction

Many have taken pen in hand to discuss the validity of C. S. Lewis's apologetic arguments. I have been one of them.[2] But in this chapter I would like to address what we can learn practically about apologetics as a part of Christian ministry from Lewis's approach to defending the faith. Lewis was not a pastor, though Providence gave him an informal pastoral role in many lives which is often on display in his letters. He was an evangelist of sorts as well as perhaps the most effective apologist the church has known. A fresh look at his approach to these two areas of ministry and how they fit together could be useful to both evangelists and apologists in the Twenty-first Century.

Evangelism

C. S. Lewis did not talk a lot about evangelism. He just did it. He often did it indirectly, but it got done. There is no direct appeal for

---

[1] C, S, Lewis, *Till We Have Faces* (1956; Grand Rapids, Mi: Eerdmans, 1968): 308.

[2] E.g. in *C. S. Lewis's Apologetics: Pro and Con*, ed. Gregory Bassham (Leiden: Brill/ Rodopi, 2015), 171–89, 201–4, and in numerous articles—not to mention here in this book!

conversion in the Broadcast Talks that became *Mere Christianity*, but there is an exposition of the Christian faith designed to elucidate its attractiveness as an answer to the problems of fallen man as well as to underscore its truth. And conversion was often the result, as famously with Charles Colson. But while Lewis's approach to evangelism may have been indirect, it was not unintentional. When Sherwood Eliot Wirt of the Billy Graham Evangelistic Association asked Lewis whether he would say that the aim of his writing was "to bring about an encounter of the reader with Jesus Christ," Lewis replied, "That is not my language, yet it is the purpose I have in view."[3] He said elsewhere that "Most of my books are evangelistic, addressed to *tous exo* ["those outside"]"[4]

Lewis did not feel he had the gifts for the "direct evangelical appeal of the 'Come to Jesus' type," but he thought that those who could do that sort of thing should "do it with all their might."[5] Lewis not only practiced evangelism by writing, but also in his speaking on the radio, speaking for the RAF in World War II, and in personal letters and other contacts. Lewis's commitment to evangelism and the price he paid for it at Oxford are covered brilliantly in the book edited by David Mills, *The Pilgrim's Guide: C. S. Lewis and the Art of Witness*, especially in the late Chris Mitchell's essay, "Bearing the Weight of Glory."[6]

Through all of these varied experiences, Lewis came to have a good understanding of some of the problems with doing effective

---

[3] C. S. Lewis, "Cross Examination," in *God in the Dock: Essays on Theology and Ethics*, ed. Walter Hooper (Grand Rapids, Mi: Eerdmans, 1970), 262.

[4] C. S. Lewis, "Rejoinder to Dr. Pittenger," in *God in the Dock*, ed. Walter Hooper (Grand Rapids, Mi: Eerdmans, 1970), 181.

[5] C. S. Lewis, "Christian Apologetics," in *God in the Dock*, ed. Walter Hooper (Grand Rapids, Mi: Eerdmans, 1970), 99.

[6] Christopher W. Mitchell, "Bearing the Weight of Glory: The Cost of C. S. Lewis's Witness," in *The Pilgrim's Guide: C. S. Lewis and the Art of Witness*, ed. David Mills (Grand Rapids, Mi: Eerdmans, 1998), 3–14.

evangelism in the modern world. One thing he noticed was that "The greatest barrier I have met is the almost total absence from the minds of my audience of any sense of sin.... We have to convince our hearers of the unwelcome diagnosis before we can expect them to welcome the news of the remedy."[7] This was a new situation without precedent in the history of the church. "When the apostles preached, they could assume even in their Pagan hearers a real consciousness of deserving the Divine anger.... Christianity now has to preach the diagnosis—in itself very bad news—before it can win a hearing for the cure."[8] This means, not an adjustment to the message, but more work for the evangelist, who can no longer do his work effectively without help from the apologist. "Christ takes it for granted that men are bad. Until we really feel this assumption of His to be true, though we are part of the world He came to save, we are not part of the audience to whom His words are addressed."[9] There is no hint of the idea that we have to adjust the message to make it more palatable to this new, tougher audience. Rather, we must gird up our loins and do the work required to gain a hearing for this unwelcome diagnosis and the joyous cure that can only make sense when it follows it.[10]

Apologetics

The evangelist increasingly needs help from the apologist because the diagnosis is no longer self-evident, and it is no longer self-ev-

---

[7] C.S. Lewis, "God in the Dock," in *God in the Dock: Essays on Theology and Ethics*, ed. Walter Hooper (Grand Rapids, Mi: Eerdmans, 1970), 243–4; cf. "Christian Apologetics," op. cit., 95.

[8] C.S. Lewis, *The Problem of Pain* (NY: MacMillan, 1967), 43.

[9] Ibid, 45.

[10] For ways to reform the church's ministry so that it can better practice biblical evangelism, see Donald T. Williams, *Ninety-Five Theses for a New Reformation: A Road Map for Post-Evangelical Christianity* (Toccoa, GA: *Semper Reformanda* Publications, 2021): 222–41.

ident partly because the Christian world view is now a foreign country to most modern people. They must be *persuaded* (the apologist's job) to try the experiment of looking at the world and their own hearts very differently from the way they habitually do if they are even to understand the relevance of the Gospel to their lives, much less accept it as Good News that is true. The "liberal" approach to this dilemma is to try to accommodate the Gospel to the modern (or now, post-modern) world view, to make it more palatable to the audience that exists. But this approach begs the question. If the Gospel is not *true*, then it is not Good News for anyone; and if it is true, then the modern world view must at points be false. Lewis does not seem to have been tempted at all by the liberal cop-out. He was fully prepared to accept the challenge that, in order to present the Good News today, we must, to an extent that was never necessary before, convince people that not just their behavior and their beliefs but their *thinking* has been mistaken at crucial points.

Apologetics is how we do this job. It is the defense of the faith, that branch of theology which asks of the Gospel, "*Why should we think it is true?*" It is the one branch of theology in which Lewis was recognized as an expert, if not a professional. His broad and deep learning, classical, philosophical, and literary, which kept him in touch with the best products of both the human mind and the human heart; his rigorous training in logic and debate by W. T. Kirkpatrick; and the fact that his own conversion was facilitated by reasoned arguments from Chesterton and Tolkien[11]: All these factors combined to make Lewis one of

---

[11] See. Donald T. Williams, "G.K. Chesterton, *The Everlasting Man*," in *C. S. Lewis's List: The Ten Books that Influenced Him Most*, ed. David Werther and Susan Werther (NY: Bloomsbury, 2015), 31–48.

the greatest apologists we have seen. What can he tell us about apologetics as a form of practical theology?

The Need for Apologetics

Apologetics is needed for many reasons. In the first place it is a biblical mandate: "Sanctify Christ as Lord in your hearts, always being ready to make a defense to everyone who asks you to give an account for the hope that is in you" (1 Pet 3.15). The word translated "defense" is ἀπολογία (*apologia*), from which we get the English word *apologetics*. It is a courtroom term which refers to the kind of reasoned case a lawyer would make in defense of his client. Lewis was in tune with a number of the reasons why that mandate exists.

One is the very nature of the faith to which the Gospel calls us. Many modern people, Christians included, treat faith as a kind of strange mystical way of knowing unconnected to reason or evidence. They treat it as a zero-sum game in which, the more reason and evidence you have for any given belief, the less of a role is left for faith to play. The New Testament, however, knows nothing of such ideas. For the New-Testament writers, faith is simply trust, and salvation is granted to people who put their personal trust in Christ as God's Messiah. "If you confess with your mouth Jesus as Lord and believe in your heart that God raised him from the dead, you shall be saved" (Rom 10.9). In Greek, the noun *faith* and the verb *I believe* are built on the same root: πίστις (*pistis*) and πιστεύω (*pisteuo*). You could conceivably have that trust for good reasons or bad reasons or no reasons. It is better to have good reasons. Luke says that Jesus offered "many convincing proofs" of his resurrection (Acts 1.3), and early preachers like the Apostle Paul were constantly giving reasons and evidence to back up their message. So we could say, as we saw in the five theses on apologetics of the introduction, that apologetics is based on a biblical precept (Peter's command), biblical precedent (the example of the Apostles), and a biblical principle (that the Gospel is *truth* that should be addressed to the whole person, including the mind).

Lewis accepted this biblical perspective fully. This acceptance is shown by his teachings on the nature of truth,[12] by his practice of apologetics, and by direct statement. "My faith is based on reason.... The battle is between faith and reason on one side and emotion and imagination on the other."[13] The idea is not that emotion and imagination are inherently opposed to faith (one factor leading to Lewis's conversion was the "baptism" of his imagination by George MacDonald), but that in fallen human beings they often are opposed to it. When reason appears to be opposed to faith, this opposition is illusory, because if the Gospel is true, then true reason must support it. We practice apologetics in our evangelism then because of the nature of the Gospel as truth and the nature of human beings as whole people who have minds as well as hearts that need to be reached.

The nature both of the Gospel and of human beings then makes apologetics a necessary part of our theology for every generation. The times in which we live can make the need even more pressing. Lewis lived in such times, and the needs he saw have not diminished since he saw them. A skeptical age will have its effects even on people raised in Christian homes. Lewis describes those effects graphically. He wrote to a Mrs. Lockley on 5 March

---

[12] See Donald T. Williams, "C. S. Lewis on Truth," in *Reflections from Plato's Cave: Essays in Evangelical Philosophy* (Lynchburg: Lantern Hollow Press, 2012), 103–28, and in *Deeper Magic*, op. cit., 23–40.

[13] C. S. Lewis, *Mere Christianity*, op. cit., 122.

1951, that "Skeptical, incredulous, materialistic *ruts* have been deeply engraved in our thought."[14] As a result, even committed Christians like Lewis have moments when Christian truth claims look implausible. What then will be the case for those without his apologetic defenses? In such an age, apologetics is essential equipment for believers wanting to preserve and strengthen their faith just as much as it is when they are proclaiming it to others.

The ruts have not only been dug; they are systematically reinforced. Lewis gives an accurate analysis of the spirit of the age:

> As long as this deliberate refusal to understand things from above, even where such understanding is possible, continues, it is idle to talk of any final victory over materialism. The critique of every experience from below, the voluntary ignoring of meaning and concentration on fact, will always have the same plausibility. There will always be evidence, and every month fresh evidence, to show that religion is only psychological, justice only self-protection, politics only economics, love only lust, and thought itself only cerebral biochemistry.[15]

The mindset Lewis is describing here is called *reductionism*: Every aspect of reality is reduced to one other thing that is held to explain it exhaustively. For the prototypical Marxist, everything is really only economics, for the Freudian, everything is really just sex, etc. For the materialist, everything is only atoms in motion, so in a materialist age various forms of reductionism will be the default setting for understanding any aspect of human experience. The reason you can always find real evidence that seems to support

[14] C.S. Lewis, *The Collected Letters of C. S. Lewis*, 3 vols., ed. Walter Hooper (San Francisco, Ca: HarperSanFrancisco 2004), 3:393.

[15] C.S. Lewis, "Transposition," sermon preached in the chapel of St. Mansfield College, Oxford, 28 May 194, in. *The Weight of Glory and Other Addresses*, ed. Walter Hooper (San Francisco, Ca: HarperCollins, 1980): 114–115.

reductionism is that thought, for example, does involve cerebral biochemistry. If you only look at it "from below," biochemistry is all you will see. But there has to be more to it than that, because if thought is reduced to brain chemistry then there is no reason to believe the thought that thought is only brain chemistry. A scientific age only accepts looking "from below" as valid looking. (Looking *from below* here would correspond to looking *at* as opposed to looking *along* in Lewis's essay "Meditation in a Toolshed."[16]) We are pounded by this mentality so consistently that it becomes one of the "ruts" Lewis spoke of. We have to make a special and concerted effort to counteract the prejudices that result from such habits of how we look at things in order to be reminded that it cannot be the whole story. Apologetics is how we make that effort.

Our age remains as skeptical as Lewis's was, and to that challenge we have now added the ruts of pluralism and its offspring multiculturalism. Lewis's ruts have been worn deeper and new ones have been added. Neither evangelism nor Christian nurture can be conducted effectively without help in navigating around, smoothing out, or bridging over those ruts. Therefore, Lewis's advice is even more pertinent today than it was when he gave it:

> To be ignorant and simple now—not to be able to meet the enemies on their own ground—would be to throw down our weapons, and to betray our uneducated brethren who have, under God, no defence but us against the intellectual attacks of the heathen. Good philosophy must exist, if for no other reason, because bad philosophy needs to be answered.[17]

---

[16] C. S. Lewis, "Meditation in a Toolshed," in *God in the Dock*, ed. Walter Hooper. (Grand Rapids, Mi: Eerdmans, 1970: 212–15.

[17] C. S. Lewis, "Learning in Wartime," sermon preached at St. Mary the Virgin, Oxford, 22 Oct. 1939, in *The Weight of Glory and Other Addresses*, ed. Walter Hooper (San Francisco, Ca: HarperCollins, 1980), 58.

Apologetic Method

Modern Christian apologists tend to group roughly into three camps in terms of methodology: Classical, Evidentialist, and Presuppositionalist. Classical apologists argue first for the existence of God, and then turn to the evidence for the resurrection of Christ to identify who that God is and how He can be known. Evidentialists differ as to how valid the classical arguments (cosmological, teleological, moral, etc.) are, but agree that they point only to an abstract God, not the God of the Bible, and so would prefer to cut to the chase and establish the historicity of the resurrection as pointing to Jesus being God incarnate. Presuppositionalists say we cannot argue *to* God, but only *from* God. In other words, our philosophical assumptions (presuppositions) determine how we are going to evaluate the evidence, and non-Christians' secular world view and rebellious hearts will not let them hear the evidence objectively and conclude that Christ is Lord. So we have to start by showing that all starting points save one (the existence of the God of the Bible) lead to contradiction. Only after we accept God as God do we have a basis for using reason to evaluate the evidence.

Increasingly people are coming to see these approaches as complementary and indeed mutually interdependent, rather than as alternative options. Unless you have reason to believe that a Creator God exists, the evidence for the resurrection of Jesus only leads to the conclusion that something really weird must have happened. Unless you see the strength of the evidence for the resurrection, the God of the classical arguments remains only an abstract theory, not a personal Savior. Analyzing the world view options and seeing the contradictions of secularism provides a context in which the evidence becomes meaningful. Presenting evidence alone surely does not lead to conversion, but presuppositionalism alone is susceptible to a charge of circularity—and no methodology is successful unless it is blessed and used by the Holy Spirit to bring about conviction and faith. And, despite the purists on all three sides, the Spirit has managed to use all three approaches in that way.

C. S. Lewis was not a part of the conversation I've summarized in the last two paragraphs, and he does not discuss the advantages and disadvantages of those approaches. He is best understood as a classical apologist who sometimes argued in ways more typical of both evidentialists and presuppositionalists. He was, in other words, an eclectic realist with some common sense. Purists in the three approaches will not find an ally in Lewis, but practical apologists will find much good advice in how to approach their task.

Lewis followed what Groothuis calls the "cumulative case approach."[18] Lewis uses many types of arguments: classical (the Moral Argument,[19] the Ontological Argument[20]), evidential (the Trilemma[21]), presuppositional (the Argument from Reason[22]), and existential (the Argument from Desire[23]). His case is not ultimately dependent on any one of them so much as on the fact that they all point to the same conclusion. He explains,

> Authority, reason, experience; on these three, mixed in varying proportions, all our knowledge depends. The authority of many wise men in many different times and places forbids me to regard the spiritual world as an illusion. My reason, showing me the ap-

[18] Douglas Groothuis, *Christian Apologetics: A Comprehensive Case for Biblical Faith* (Downers Grove, Il.: Intervarsity Press, 2022), 41f, 52f..

[19] See chapter one of this book.

[20] See chapter two of this book.

[21] See chapter four of this book.

[22] See chapter three of this book.

[23] See chapter five of this book.

parently insoluble difficulties of materialism and proving that the hypothesis of a spiritual world covers far more of the facts with far fewer assumptions, forbids me again. My experience even of such feeble attempts as I have made to live the spiritual life does not lead to the results which the pursuit of an illusion ordinarily leads to, and therefore forbids me yet again.[24]

Authority, reason, experience: When they agree, one can proceed with a certain amount of confidence.

Practical Apologetics
There are then a number of arguments pointing to the truth of the Christian faith, some of them quite strong. But Lewis realized that having good arguments is not enough. We also need to influence the general climate of opinion. In a secular age, unexamined attitudes and ideas influence our minds in ways that do not affect the validity of the reasons we have always had for believing in God, but may have a powerful effect on their plausibility. For example, Elwin Ransom of the Space Trilogy insists that "What we need for the moment is not so much a body of belief as a body of people familiarized with certain ideas. If we could even effect in one per cent of our readers a change-over from the conception of Space to the conception of Heaven, we should have made a beginning."[25] Space is a vast unpopulated emptiness in which life is an anomaly; heaven is a vibrant matrix of being pulsating with life and light. How we imagine the world has an influence on how we think about it, the kinds of arguments we will be drawn to, and the kind of conclusions we will draw about it.

---

[24] C.S. Lewis, "Religion: Reality or Substitute?" in *Christian Reflections*, ed. Walter Hooper (Grand Rapids, Mi: Eerdmans, 1967), 41.

[25] C.S. Lewis, *Out of the Silent Planet* (NY: Simon & Schuster Inc., 1996), 154.

Lewis's arguments were effective then partly because he knew that more than argument was needed. In Lewis's apologetic, they were supplemented by attempts to imagine what the world would look like if Christianity were true as well as arguments that were not directly about apologetic issues. Lewis wanted Christians to pursue intellectual excellence in general in order to create a situation in which people were not so unused to seeing things from the perspective of the Christian world view as they were already becoming in his generation. "What we want," he said, "is not more little books about Christianity, but more little books by Christians on other subjects."[26] When the best available treatments of art, literature, politics, philosophy, ethics, science, etc. all speak as if Christianity were true (without directly mentioning it), then when the time comes to make the case for its truth directly, a receptive audience will have been created. We have much work left to do in this area.

Lewis was also an effective apologist because he was winsome and intelligent. One of my favorite passages is one in which he slyly turns the tables on the skeptics. As an atheist, Lewis had had to believe that the great majority of the human race was wrong; "When I became a Christian," he remarks, "I was able to take a more liberal view."[27] Here he steals a favorite buzz word, "liberal," and a favorite stance, that of tolerant open-mindedness, from his opponents, and stands them on their heads to be used against them. Who is really open minded? Lewis makes his point, but he doesn't rub it in; he makes it and moves on. We could learn a lot from him in manner as well as in message.

Lewis had a unique gift for being able to express the most profound Christian ideas that apologetics needs to defend in lan-

---

[26] "Christian Apologetics," op. cit., 93.
[27] *Mere Christianity*, op. cit., 43.

guage that normal human beings can understand. This was a gift, but it is also a skill that can be cultivated. Lewis wrote to John Beddow on 7 Oct. 1945, "It has always seemed to me odd that those who are sent to evangelise the Bantus begin by learning Bantu while the Church turns out annually curates to teach the English who simply don't know the vernacular language of England."[28] He also stressed that you do not really even understand a concept if you cannot translate it into the vernacular. He thought such translation ought to be a compulsory paper for every ordination examination.[29] It was good advice for the apologist as well as the pastor and the evangelist. Sadly, today in Academia, in the humanities at least, there is a prejudice to the effect that writing cannot be intellectual if it is intelligible. Lewis's entire corpus gives the lie to that erroneous notion. It would be good if a host of theologians and apologists following his example could give the lie to it too.

Lewis was also careful not to claim too much. He gives multiple arguments to the best explanation and does not typically claim to have a slam-dunk proof. He wrote to Sheldon Vanauken on 23 Dec. 1950, "I do not think there is a *demonstrative* proof (like Euclid) of Christianity, nor of the existence of matter, nor of the good will & honesty of my best & oldest friends. I think all three are... far more probable than the alternatives."[30] Not only does this approach relieve us of the burden of trying to prove more than we can, but it is also consistent with the nature of the response we are looking for. As Lewis further explained, God does not give us a demonstrative proof, not because it would take faith off the table

---

[28] *Collected Letters*, op. cit., 2:674.
[29] "Christian Apologetics," op. cit., 98–99.
[30] *Collected Letters*, op. cit., 3:75.

by rendering faith and reason a zero-sum game, but because a response of mere intellectual assent is not what He is after.

> Are *we* interested in it in personal matters? I demand from my friend trust in my good faith which is certain without demonstrative proof. It wouldn't be confidence at all if he waited for rigorous proof. Hang it all, the very fairy tales embody the truth. Othello believed in Desdemona's innocence when it was proved. ... Lear believed in Cordelia's love when it was proved: but that was too late."[31]

Faith—personal trust—is not indifferent to evidence. But we do not value faith very highly when it is given only if there is no intellectual alternative, or when it wavers with every fluctuation in the ebb and flow of circumstances. Apologetics is not about creating indubitable certainty but about enabling and supporting a well-warranted personal trust. It will be healthier and more effective to the extent that we remember this.

The Final Apologetic
Lewis would have agreed with Francis Schaeffer that "the final apologetic" is a life lived as if the Christian message were true.[32] Lewis noted, "If Christianity should happen to be true, then it is quite impossible that those who know this truth and those who don't should be equally well equipped for leading a good life."[33] Christians so equipped should indeed be leading a life that not only exhibits human thriving from the application of Christian truths but also a sacrificial commitment to showing the love of

---

[31] Ibid.

[32] Francis Schaeffer, *The God Who is There: Speaking Historic Christianity into the Twentieth Century* (Downers Grove, Il.: Inter-Varsity Press, 1958, 152; cf. *The Mark of the Christian* (Downers Grove, IL.: Inter-Varsity Press, 1970).

[33] C.S. Lewis, "Man or Rabbit?" in *God in the Dock: Essays on Theology and Ethics*, ed. Walter Hooper (Grand Rapids, Mi: Eerdmans, 1970), 109.

Christ to each other and to the world. Without this "final apologetic," no argument will be compelling to people from whom we are asking not just intellectual assent but life commitment. And to some, it will be the only argument that can speak. As Lewis wrote to a Miss Gladding on 7 June 1945, "When a person... has lost faith under so very great and bewildering a trial, no intellectual approach is likely to avail. But where people can resist and ignore arguments, they may be unable to resist *lives.*"[34]

The final practical point is the realization that apologetics is a form of spiritual warfare, and not one without casualties. The best way to be one of those casualties is to ignore the danger. Lewis did not. He realized that "Nothing is more dangerous to one's own faith than the work of the apologist. No doctrine of that faith seems to me so spectral, so unreal, as the one I have just successfully defended.... For a moment, you see, it has seemed to rest on oneself."[35] Therefore it is indispensable that we have a serious reckoning with the fact that intellectual preparation is necessary but not enough. The apologist must be a person who walks with the Lord in such a way that he cannot forget on Whom things truly rest.

Application

Why do we need apologetics? We live in a world filled with people who think like Trumpkin: "I have no use for magic lions which are talking lions and don't talk, and friendly lions though they don't do us any good, and whopping big lions though nobody can see them."[36] The only cure for that attitude was for Trumpkin

---

[34] *Collected Letters*, op. cit., 2:659.
[35] "Christian Apologetics," op. cit., 103).
[36] C. S. Lewis, *Prince Caspian* (NY: HarperCollins, 1979), 156.

actually to meet Aslan. Well, we are all of us constitutionally un-believing Narnian dwarfs. "You see," said Aslan. "They will not let us help them. They have chosen cunning instead of belief. Their prison is only in their own minds, yet they are in that prison; and are so afraid of being taken in that they cannot be taken out."[37]

Only the Holy Spirit can take us out of ourselves, out of those internal prisons, to the point that we can hear the evidence for Christ and respond to it with faith. But the Spirit wants us to be ready and able to present that evidence when He does so. Lewis's friend Austin Farrer put it well: "Though argument does not create conviction, the lack of it destroys belief. What seems to be proved may not be embraced; but what no one shows the ability to defend is quickly abandoned. Rational argument does not create belief, but it maintains a climate in which belief can flourish."[38]

Lewis, in other words, well understood that the goal of apologetics is not just to win arguments. It must be what he allowed to Sherwood Eliot Wirt was the goal of all his writing: "to bring about an encounter of the reader with Jesus Christ," the kind of encounter Lewis described so well: "There comes a moment when people who have been dabbling in religion ('Man's search for God') suddenly draw back. Supposing we really found him? We never meant it to come to that! Worse still, supposing he found us?"[39]

The purpose of apologetics then is to help people channel the shock of that encounter into a serious consideration of the claims of Christ. It is to ensure that this encounter is with the Christ of history and not a counterfeit, that it is an encounter of the whole person with that Christ, and that the faith we hope these

---

[37] C.S. Lewis, *The Last Battle* (NY: HarperCollins, 1984), 185–6.

[38] Austin Farrer, "The Christian Apologist," in *Light on C. S. Lewis*, ed. Jocelyn Gibb (NY: Harcourt, Brace, & World, 1965), 26.

[39] C.S. Lewis, *Miracles: A Preliminary Study* (NY: MacMillan, 1947), 96–7.

people will put in Him will be a rational and well-considered and well-grounded faith. It is to help believers whose faith is more fragmented and superficial grow into that rational, well-considered, and well-grounded faith themselves so that they may be preserved in it.[40] It is to remind them in their inevitable moments of doubt that faith is "the art of holding onto things your reason has once accepted, in spite of your changing moods."[41]

The goal is not just to win arguments. It matters little that we persuade people that theism is true in the abstract unless this enables them to meet God. Lewis reminds us, "We trust not because 'a God' exists, but because *this* God exists."[42] We want to get people to the place where "What would, a moment before, have been variations in opinion, now become variations in your personal attitude to a Person. You are no longer faced [simply] with an argument which demands your assent, but with a Person who demands your confidence."[43] For if indeed they can be brought to see the glory of God in the face of Jesus Christ, they will be ready to say with Orual, "You are yourself the answer. Before your face questions die away."[44]

---

[40] For ways to reform the church's ministry so that it can better foster such healthy faith in its Christian nurture, see Donald T. Williams, *Ninety-Five Theses for a New Reformation, op. cit.*, 146–64, 312–48, 372–406.

[41] *Mere Christianity*, op. cit., 123.n

[42] C. S. Lewis, "On Obstinacy in Belief," in *The World's Last Night and other Essays* (NY: Harcourt, Brace & World, 1960), 25.

[43] Ibid., 26.

[44] C. S. Lewis, *Till We Have Faces: A Myth Retold* (Harcourt Brace & World, 1956; rpt. Grand Rapids, Mi: Eerdmans, 1968), 308.

INTERLUDE

PRESCRIPTION FOR A BROKEN RELATIONSHIP

The Heart has reasons Reason doesn't know.
    If either from the other looks away,
        There is no way the person can be whole.
Though we must always pay the debts we owe
    And Reason has a voice we must obey,
        The Heart has reasons Reason doesn't know.
Though she may sometimes feel like Reason's foe,
    The Heart must turn to him and sweetly say,
        "As enemies, we never can be whole."
On hearing this, he must not gloat or crow,
    But grace with grace and courtesy repay:
        The Heart has reasons Reason doesn't know.
When we have fallen, shattered bones may grow
    Back crooked; they cannot be left that way.
        We have to break them then to make them whole.
The sad condition of the human soul
    Needs nothing less its conflicts to allay.
        The Heart has reasons Reason doesn't know,
And only what is broken can be whole

CHAPTER NINE

"Bluspels and Flalansferes"
The Role of Imagination in Lewis's Rational Apologetic

"After the storm there's a rainbow,
And all of the colors are black.
It's not that the colors aren't there;
It's just imagination we lack
In my little town."[1]

One of the reasons C.S. Lewis is uniquely important as a Christian thinker and apologist is the way he integrates reason and imagination in his expository writings as well as his fiction, all in the service of truth.[2] But what is truth? Pilate's cynical question still demands an answer, and Lewis's is especially helpful because of the way it calls both Reason and Imagination into a coordinated team working under Truth as their captain. So how did Lewis answer that question, and what does imagination contribute? It is more than just letting him write good stories to illustrate the truths he wants to communicate.

---

[1] "My Little Town," pop song by Paul Simon.
[2] For a treatment of the many ways in which Lewis uses imagination, see Root and Neal, *The Surprising Imagination of C. S, Lewis*, op cit.

Lewis's Understanding of Imagination

Lewis is solidly in the mainstream of Christian thinking about truth.[3] Truth is a property of propositions such that they correspond with the state of affairs in the objective world that they purport to describe. Augustine and Aquinas, Calvin and Wesley, Cardinal Newman and Carl F. H. Henry would all have affirmed the same basic points, though not perhaps with Lewis's characteristically deft use of apt analogy. What Lewis adds to the discussion is some careful thinking about the relations of truth not o to reason but also to imagination. It was his experience and his conviction that "All things, in their way, reflect heavenly truth, imagination not least."[4] How exactly does imagination do so?

Some of Lewis's interpreters, influenced perhaps by the surface resemblance in language between Lewis and the English Romantics, have not paid sufficiently careful attention to the way Lewis answers that question. One reads statements such as "Lewis, like many Romantics, intuitively trusted the capacity of imagination to be a 'faculty of truth.'"[5]

What Lewis actually said when he analyzed the relation between imagination and truth was much more carefully and rigorously thought out:

> We are not talking about truth but meaning: meaning which is the antecedent condition of both truth and falsehood, whose antithesis is not error but nonsense. I am a rationalist. For me, reason is the natural organ of truth; but imagination is the organ of

---

[3] For a more complete treatment, see Donald T. Williams, *Deeper Magic: The Theology behind the Writings of C. S. Lewis*, op. cit., 26–40.

[4] Lewis, *Surprised by Joy*, op. cit., 167.

[5] Eliane Tixier, "Imagination Baptized," *The Longing for a Form: Essays on the Fiction of C. S. Lewis*, ed. Peter J. Schackel (Grand Rapids, Mi: Baker, 1971): 141.

meaning. Imagination, producing new metaphors or revivifying old, is not the cause of truth, but its condition.[6]

Imagination is the faculty or organ not of truth (directly) but of *meaning*, which is the "antecedent condition" of truth. What does this mean?

Suppose I utter the proposition, "Blepple hloisats kleply flarg krunk bluzzles," and then ask you for a verdict on its truth or falsehood. Say, what? I suspect you would be somewhat handicapped in trying to render that verdict by the minor problem that you would have no idea what I had said. Before you could even begin to form a judgment on the truth question, you would need to know what a hloisat is, how a blepple one differs from a regular one, what it is to flarg, what a bluzzle is, what is the quality of krunkness, and how flarging kleply differs from regular flarging. In order to give you that information I would have to render these objects, qualities, and actions in concrete terms that you could visualize. Your Imagination would be the faculty that enabled you to form a picture—an image—of what the proposition is asserting (or whether it is asserting anything). Then your Reason could compare that mental picture to the picture of reality it has already tested and come to trust, in order to see if correspondence or contradiction resulted.

Imagination, in other words, doesn't give us truth. *Reason* for Lewis is the organ of truth. Just because we can imagine something does not make it real. But Imagination combined with Reason can give us *meaningful* truth, truth that impacts us on other levels than mere academic intellectual assent. This is truth that can appeal to head and heart together. Lewis was the master of

---

[6] C.S. Lewis, "Bluspels and Flalansferes: A Semantic Nightmare," *Selected Literary Essays*, ed. Walter Hooper (Cambridge: Cambridge Univ. Pr., 1969): 265.

giving it to us, whether in his expository prose or his fiction. The hall and rooms of a house for the church and its denominations; two books which have always been resting one on the other for the eternal generation of the Son; the keys of a piano and a tune for the relationship between our instincts and the moral law; entrusting oneself to the waves and floating islands of Perelandra rather than sleeping on the fixed land for faith; the Stone Table for the Law and Aslan's death cracking it for the Gospel; Puddlegum the Marshwiggle for dogged faithfulness and Reepicheep the Mouse for valor, chivalry, and honor: The brilliant artistic construction of these images does not prove that they are images of truth. But their presence in the context of the linear arguments and narrative trajectories of which they are parts makes the truths established by those lines of development *mean* something; it makes their impact, their beauty, and their relevance easier to see *and to feel*.

Mythology for Lewis was one of the most important places where this contribution of imagination to our ability to grasp the meaning of true (or false) propositions is seen. It is well known that for Lewis myth was not the opposite of truth, as it is in popular usage, but rather one way in which truth can be conveyed or embodied. Myth is not necessarily composed of "lies breathed through silver" (as the pre-conversion Lewis once foolishly said to Tolkien) but can be "a real though unfocused gleam of divine truth falling on human imagination."[7]

Myth may then convey these truths to the imaginations of readers, who might then independently verify them through reason and hence validly accept them as true. Thus George MacDonald's modern mythic stories helped move Lewis in the direction

---

[7] Lewis, *Miracles* 1947, op. cit., 139n.

of Christian faith by giving a meaning to the concept of holiness, even as Lewis's own stories have done for countless readers since. The mythical quality of the story refers in Lewis's usage to its meaningfulness rather than its truth or falsehood as such, which must be established on other grounds. Hence Lewis could without contradiction refer to the New Testament story of Jesus' birth, death, and resurrection as "myth become fact."[8]

Lewis is careful to use this language correctly even in his fiction. "Long since on Mars, and more strongly since he came to Perelandra, Ransom had been perceiving that the triple distinction of truth from myth and both from fact was purely terrestrial—was part and parcel of that unhappy division between soul and body that resulted from the Fall."[9] "Fact" in this passage is the bit of reality that truth is about; "truth" the account that corresponds to that reality; "myth" the story that allows us to taste the particular tang of that fact. Ransom experiences in Perelandra the pre-analytical unity that lies behind the differentiated categories.

When one is inside a myth, in other words—say, on Perelandra with Ransom or in Narnia with the Pevensies—one experiences the unified reality from which all three— fact, truth, and myth— flow. When talking about that experience later, one has perforce to use the differentiated language, and Lewis does so consistently. He was doing so even in his earliest Christian fiction: "Child, if you will, it is mythology. It is but truth, not fact; an image, not the very real."[10] A true statement about reality is not reality; not even a mythical statement is reality; but it may be true nonetheless, i.e., it may correspond in a faithful manner to the reality it describes.

[8] C. S. Lewis, "Myth Become Fact," op. cit., 67.

[9] C. S. Lewis, *Perelandra* (1943; NY: Scribner, 1996): 143–4, cf. "Myth Become Fact," op. cit., 66.

[10] Lewis, *Pilgrim's Regress*, op. cit., 171.

Because the meaningful creating and sustaining acts of a personal, purposeful, and rational God are the ultimate source of all reality, there is indeed a real unity between fact and truth, and between both and myth, the most meaningful statement of truth. And some of this meaning may be stated propositionally, and some of those propositions may be confirmed by Reason as true.

Lewis then embraces the traditional and standard correspondence theory of truth and enriches it by relating truth to imagination and myth. To recapitulate: Truth is a property of accounts or propositions such that their assertions correspond with reality. Imagination is the organ of meaning, the antecedent condition of truth or falsehood, i.e., of the meaningfulness of those accounts claiming to be true or false. Reason, which distinguishes and discerns correspondence or non-correspondence (between those propositions and each other, between them and reality) and pursues their implications, is the organ of truth. Myth is a story that enables the imagination to receive and taste ways of seeing the world that reason can then confirm as true or false.

Lewis's Use of Imagination

So how do we apply these concepts apologetically in our own proclamation of the Gospel? Well, how did Lewis apply them? He did it by doing in prose what Dr. Johnson said was the purpose of poetry: it is "the art of uniting pleasure with truth by calling imagination to the help of reason."[11] The best way to understand that is to think about some of the examples we mentioned above.

Lewis does not limit his use of imagination to his fiction. It is the faculty that enables him to create such perfect analogies and

---

[11] Samuel Johnson, *The Lives of the Poets: Milton*, in *Samuel Johnson: Rasselas, Poems, and Selected Prose*, 3rd ed., ed. Bertrand H. Bronson (San Francisco, Ca: Rhinehart, 1971): 238.

word pictures for the concepts he tries to explain in his expository prose. The hall and rooms of a house as a picture of the church and its denominations is one of his more famous analogies. If you want to write about "mere" Christianity and have people relate to it properly, how do you achieve this? You want them to appreciate what all Christians have in common, but also to be loyal to a particular local church and its larger denominational family. Well, let your readers imagine a long central hall with rooms off either side. The rooms are unified by the hall as part of the same house. It is good to be in the house; at least you are out of the rain. But camping in the hall is rather awkward. It is *in the rooms* that there are fires and meals and conversation. Your imagination is what lets you picture the house and explore it and think about its implications. It is what lets you know what it means to be a part of a Room that is part of that House.

Of course, Lewis's most memorable uses of this technique are found in his fiction. The floating islands of Perelandra are arresting images in themselves, creating a landscape different from all those we know because it is ever changing. But then that picture turns out to be central to the plot of the novel, which has to do with the temptation of the Adam and Eve of that new world. The "forbidden fruit" of Perelandra is sleeping on the fixed land, as opposed to the floating islands. Why? Because that would imply an assertion of your own will to fix your own destiny rather than accepting the gift of what Maleldil sends you on the next wave. On the fixed land you wake up where you went to sleep; on a floating island you might be anywhere the next morning. You can have either a security of your own making, or a life of faith. Make your choice! The picture as imagined lets us understand what faith and trust and obedience really are and transfer that understanding to the real world.

Many of us have heard about Jesus dying on the Cross to pay for our sins so many times that we have been anesthetized to it. But when Aslan the great Lion allows himself to be slaughtered on the Stone Table by the White Witch in place of the traitor Edmund, a couple of things happen. For one, our guard is down. Lewis explains what he was up to this way:

> I saw how stories of this kind could steal past a certain inhibition which had paralyzed much of my own religion in childhood. Why did one find it so hard to feel as one was told one ought to feel about God or about the sufferings of Christ? I thought that the chief reason was that one was told one ought to.... But supposing that by casting all these things into an imaginary world, stripping them of their stained-glass and Sunday school associations, one could make them for the first time appear in their real potency? Could one not thus steal past those watchful dragons?[12]

Many people are prepared to testify that, yes, one could, for Lewis did.

The second thing that happens is that, whether our watchful dragons needed to be snuck past or not, we see the old familiar story all over again, in a new light. The very freshness of these new images re-engages our imaginations to realize afresh what it means for an innocent victim to be sacrificed out of love. Details that are parallel not only remind us of what we knew about the original story but also create the opportunity to see new aspects of the meaning they always had. The shaving of Aslan's mane for the brutality and humiliation leading up to the actual crucifixion,

---

[12] C. S. Lewis, "Sometimes Fairy Stories May Say Best What's to be Said," *Of Other World: Essays and Stories*, ed. Waler Hooper (NY: Harcourt Brace Jovanovich, 1966): 37.

the grief of Lucy and Susan for the gravity of what was sacrificed, the cracking of the Stone Table at Aslan's resurrection for the breaking of the power of the Law to condemn us: All these details allow our imaginations to enter anew into the depths of the meaning of the biblical story.

Application

Two points then in closing. First, has anyone noticed that we have seen this approach before? It is the very same teaching technique that Jesus used in his parables, which create vivid imaginative pictures to convey the Lord's theological points. We should appeal to imagination as well as to reason not just because it works, not just because it worked for Lewis, but because we have an even greater and more authoritative example than his to follow.

Second, I hope you will realize that I am not just exhorting you to use more and better illustrations. How many times have we come away from a sermon or a Sunday-School lesson remembering the illustration or the story but not the point it was supposed to be illustrating, much less the logical structure of the argument in which that point was imbedded? That doesn't happen with Lewis or Jesus, though, does it? Does anybody not remember what the Prodigal Son or the Sower and the Seed or the Good Samaritan were about? Does anybody remember Reepiceep's courage or Puddleglum's dogged faithfulness and not remember why they mattered? Has anyone forgotten what the undragoning of Eustace was really about?

Now, surely someone is going to say, "Wait a minute!" Doesn't Jesus say that the purpose of His parables was to *prevent* understanding? He speaks to the masses in parables "*in order that* 'seeing they may not see and hearing they may not understand'"

(Luke 8.10, emphasis added). That statement confused me for a long time, because it is obvious that the parables in fact function for us just as I described above. *For us*: that is the crucial piece that makes the puzzle come together. The parables did not prevent the *disciples* from understanding, because they asked for and received the key to their interpretation. Those, on the other hand, who were willing to stop just with the story and not concern themselves with its meaning were allowed to do so. Let's not be those people, and let's not give our own students or parishioners an excuse to be, either.

So the parables do promote meaningful understanding for those who receive them in the light of their role in the context of the logically structured argument I spoke of at the beginning—for those, in other words, who are willing to participate in the conversation that Jesus' integrated use of both reason and imagination is designed to enable. But stories that are less imaginatively integrated into that structure do not. What's the difference? Jesus and Lewis did not just use their imaginations alongside their reason. What they model for us is the full *integration* of imagination and reason. Illustrations and stories can't just be decorations added on; they must flow from a deep understanding of the content. This is a skill. It cannot be taken for granted. But it can be learned. We can improve at it. How? By paying attention to Jesus and to people like Lewis, not only in terms of their content but also their *method*. This will mean thinking their content through thoroughly *and* imagining it through. Start with Jesus' parables and Lewis's word pictures. Picture them in your mind as actually being played out. Meditate on that as well as on the abstract point being conveyed.

Then use that technique in the communication of your own apologetic—having first made sure that the logical structure of the argument your word pictures illustrate *is* logical. And then let them not so much illustrate it as incarnate it.

Maybe that is part of what it means to be a disciple.

INTERLUDE

THERE THEN ABIDE THESE THREE
For Father Ronald Murphy

And what is Faith? Not simply to believe
    Unless Hope is no more than wishful thinking
    Or Love a cynical disguise for lust.
Evidence and reason can relieve
    All valid doubt, and yet still leave us shrinking
    From what we do not love and will not trust.

Reason is necessary, not enough.
    Soul-conquering Love must come alongside, linking
    The mind in Hope to One who felt the thrust
Of all our hate and still looked back in love.
    In *Him* we trust.

CONCLUSION

C. S. Lewis is still the dean of Christian apologists. A good case can be made that he was simply the greatest of all modern apologists. Why would we say that? He did not have more philosophical rigor than a William Lane Craig or a Norm Geisler. He did not have the background in legal reasoning of a John Warwick Montgomery or the experience in forensic analysis of a J. Warner Wallace. He did not have the knowledge of the ins and outs of New-Testament criticism that a Lydia McGrew has acquired to go along with her background in analytic philosophy or the scientific expertise of a John Lennox. He did not have the prophetic voice of a Francis Schaeffer or the comprehensiveness of a Douglas Groothuis. But he combined a measure of good many of those virtues with a popular appeal that even Lee Strobel and Greg Koukl cannot match. He practiced a level of the integration of reason and imagination that the rest of us can only dream about. And as I said in the chapter on the Trilemma above, his unique combination of wide learning, no-nonsense clarity, elegant language, and apt analogy remains the standard to which we should all aspire and the example we should seek to emulate. While some of the other fine apologists in this paragraph have seen further in their particular area of expertise, I think most of them would say that they have done so, in part, by standing on Lewis's shoulders.

If you have read this book, it is probably because you had come to appreciate Lewis's work already. Introducing others to Lewis's works can still be a useful service, but more care is needed in doing that than we might think. The uneducated British laymen who were the audience for *Mere Christianity* had a far greater ability to follow a linear argument than most of the college students I taught in recent years. The dumbing down of curricula and the evisceration of attention spans we have seen in just the last generation mean that even C.S. Lewis, that great popularizer who explained Christian ideas to the masses, will now himself need go-betweens to mediate between his writings and much of the general public. I hope reading this book will help to put you in a position the better to perform that needed task, even as it shows why it is needed.

And why is it needed? Lewis had the gift of enabling people who are not professional academics to think on a level that would otherwise have been inaccessible to them. He can still do that for some. He also lets those of us who have some academic training make more and better use of it than we could have made without his help. These gifts, combined with the excellence of his apologetic and literary works in their own right, make him the place to start in learning to do apologetics, even now that many of his seminal works are eight decades old. But while Lewis is still a good place to start, he was never a good place to stop. He is less so now than ever, due to that passage of time. So we have tried to bring out the virtues of his arguments and highlight what we can learn from them about doing our own apologetic in our own voice for our own times.

Our own apologetic in our own voice for our own times: If Lewis could have imagined in his life that almost a century later, he would still be helping us with that, he would have been astonished. And if he could have believed it, I think he would have been pleased. And so, I believe, would his Lord.

Let us please Him.

POSTLUDE

APOLOGIA

Structured steps within the Dance,
Things which could not be by chance:
Architecture of belief?
Arch of bole and vein of leaf.
Crystal's angles; raindrop's curves;
Bone and sinew knit with nerves.
Flick of wrist, fly-toss, and then,
Break of bubble, flash of fin.
Beyond these sure and certain hints,
A clearer class of evidence:
Broken fever; opened eyes;
Dove descending from the skies.
Footstep firm on slope of wave;
Stone rolled back from Jesus' grave.
Glory growing out of grief?
Architecture of belief.
Things which could not be by chance:
Structured steps within the Dance.

BIBLIOGRAPHY

Aeschliman, Michael D. *The Restitution of Man: C. S. Lewis and the Case against Scientism.* Grand Rapids, Mi: Eerdmans, 1983; rpt. 1998.

Anscombe, Elizabeth. "S. S. Lewis's Rewrite of Chapter III of *Miracles,*" *C. S. Lewis and His Circle: Essays and Memoirs from the Oxford C. S. Lewis Society,* ed. Roger White, Judith Wolfe, and Brendan Wolfe. Oxford: Oxford University Press, 2015: 14–23.

Anselm. "Proslogium." *Basic Writings.* Trans. S. N. D. Deane. LaSalle, IL: Open Court, 1903: 1–34.

Baggett, David. "Pro: The Moral Argument is Convincing." *C. S. Lewis's Christian Apologetics: Pro and Con.* Ed. Gregory Bassham. Leiden: Rodopi, 2015: 121–140.

Baggett, David, Gary R. Habermas, and Jerry L. Walls, eds. *C. S. Lewis as Philosopher: Truth, Goodness, and Beauty..* Downers Grove, IL: InterVarsity Press, 2008.

Barfield, Owen. *Owen Barfield on C. S. Lewis.* ed. G. B. Tennyson. Middletown, Ct: Wesleyan Univ. Pr., 1989.

Barratt, David. *C. S. Lewis and his World.* Grand Rapids, Mi: Eerdmans, 1987.

Bassham, Gregory, ed. *C. S. Lewis's Apologetics: Pro and Con.* Leiden: Brill/Rodopi, 2015.

_____. "Con: Quenching the Argument from Desire." *C. S. Lewis's Christian Apologetics: Pro and Con.* Ed. Gregory Bassham. Leiden: Rodopi, 2015: 45–55.

_____. "Reply to Peter S. Williams." *C. S. Lewis's Christian Apologetics: Pro and Con*. Ed. Gregory Bassham. Leiden: Rodopi, 2015: 69–74

Bauckham, Richard. *Jesus and the Eyewitnesses: The Gospels as Eyewitness Testimony*. Grand Rapids, Mi: Eerdmans, & Cambridge: Cambridge University Press, 2006.

Beversluis, John. *C. S. Lewis and the Search for Rational Religion*. Grand Rapids, Mi: Eerdmans, 1985.

_____. *C. S. Lewis and the Search for Rational Religion*. Revised and Updated. Amherst, NY: Prometheus Books, 2007.

Boruch, A. "Logical Terms, Glossary of." *The Encyclopedia of Philosophy*. New York, NY: MacMillan, 1967: 5:57.

Brazier, P. H. *C. S. Lewis: The Work of Christ Revealed*. Vol. 2 of *C. S. Lewis: Revelation and the Christ*. Eugene, Or: Pickwick, 2012.

Brown, Devin. *A Life Observed: A Spiritual Biography of C. S. Lewis*. Grand Rapids, Mi: Brazos Press, 2013.

Bruce, F.F. *The New Testament Documents: Are They Reliable?* Downers Grove, Il;: Inter-Varsity Press, 1960.

Burson, Scott R. & Jerry L. Walls. *C. S. Lewis and Francis Schaeffer: Lessons for a New Century from the Most Influential Apologists of our Time*. Downers Grove, Il: InterVarsity Press, 1998.

Carpenter, Humphrey. *The Inklings*. Boston, Ma: Houghton Mifflin, 1979.

Campbell-Jack, W. C. and Gavin McGrath, eds. *New Dictionary of Christian Apologetics*. Downers Grove, Il: InterVarsity Press, 2006.

Chesterton, G.K. *The Everlasting Man*. New York, NY: Dodd, Mead, & Company, 1925.

Christopher, Joe R. *C. S. Lewis*. Twayne's English Authors Series. Boston, Ma: G.K. Hall, 1987.

Clark, David G. *C. S. Lewis: A Guide to his Theology*. Oxford: Blackwell, 2007.

Craig, William Lane. *Reasonable Faith: Christian Truth and Apologetics*. Wheaton, Il: Crossway, 1984.

Cunningham, Richard B. *C. S. Lewis: Defender of the Faith*. Philadelphia, Pa: Westminster Press, 1967.

Davis, Stephen T. "The Mad/Bad/God Trilemma: A Reply to Daniel Howard-Snyder." *Faith and Philosophy* 21:4 (Oct. 2004): 480–92.

Eadmer. *The Life of Anselm, Archbishop of Canterbury*. Ed. with Introduction, Notes, and Translation by R. W. Southern. Oxford: Clarendon Press, 1962.

Edwards, Bruce L., Jr., ed. *C. S. Lewis: Life, Works, Legacy*, 4 vols. London: Praeger, 2007.

_____. *A Rhetoric of Reading: C. S. Lewis's Defense of Western Literacy*. Provo, Utah: Center for the Study of Christian Values in Literature, 1986.

Farrer. Austin. "The Christian Apologist." *Light on C. S. Lewis*, ed. Jocelyn Gibb. New York, NY: Harcourt, Brace, & World, 1965: 23–43.

Gilbert, Douglas and Clyde S. Kilby, *C. S. Lewis: Images of his World*. Grand Rapids, Mi: Eerdmans, 1973.

Goffar, Janine. *The C. S. Lewis Index: A Comprehensive Guide to Lewis's Writings and Ideas*. Wheaton, Il: Crossway, 1998.

Grahame, Kenneth. *The Wind in the Willows*. Illustrated by Tasha Todor. 1908; rpt. Cleveland, Oh: The World Publishing Co., 1966.

Green, Roger Lancelyn & Walter Hooper. *C. S. Lewis: A Biography*. New York, NY: Harcourt Brace Jovanovich, 1974.

Groothuis, Douglas. *Christian Apologetics: A Comprehensive Case for Biblical Faith*. Downers Grove, Il: Intervarsity Press, 2011.

_____. *Christian Apologetics: A Comprehensive Case for Biblical Faith* 2nd ed. Downers Grove, Il: InterVarsity Press, 2022.

_____. *Truth Decay: Defending Christianity against the Challenges of Postmodernism*. Downers Grove, IL: InterVarsity Press, 2000.

Hackett, Stuart C. *The Resurrection of Theism: Prolegomena to Christian Apology*. Grand Rapids, Mi: Baker, 1957.

J. B. S. Haldane, "When I am Dead," *Possible Worlds and Other Essays*. London: Charto & Windus, 1927: 209.

Hinten, Marvin D. "Approaches to Teaching Mere Christianity." *The Lamp-Post of the Southern California C. S. Lewis Society*, 30:2 (Summer 2006, pub. April 2008): 3–11.

Holmes, Michael W., ed. *The Apostolic Fathers: Greek Texts and English Translations of their Writings*. Grand Rapids, Mi: Baker, 1992.

Hooper, Walter, ed. *The Collected Letters of C. S. Lewis*, 3 vol. San Francisco, Ca: HarperSanFrancisco, 2004.

Horner, David A. "*Aut Deus aut Malus Homo*: A Defense of C. S. Lewis's 'Shocking Alternative.'" *C. S. Lewis as Philosopher: Truth, Goodness, and Beauty*. Ed. David Baggett, Gary Habermas, and Jerry L. Walls. Downers Grove, Il: IVP Academic, 2008: 68–84.

Howard-Snyder, Daniel. "Was Jesus Mad, Bad, or God?... Or Merely Mistaken?" *Faith and Philosophy* 21:4 (Oct. 2004): 456–79.

Johnson, David Kyle. "Con: Naturalism Undefeated." *C. S. Lewis's Apologetics: Pro and Con*. Ed. Gregory Bassham. Leiden: Brill/Rodopi, 2015: 91–103.

Johnson, Samuel. *The Lives of the Poets: Milton*, in *Samuel Johnson: Rasselas, Poems, and Selected Prose*, 3rd ed. Ed. Bertrand H. Bronson. San Francisco, Ca: Rhinehart, 1971: 331–52.

Kilby, Clyde S. *The Christian World of C. S. Lewis*. Grand Rapids, Mi: Eerdmans, 1964.

Koukl, Greg. *Tactics: A Game Plan for Discussing Your Christian Convictions*. Grand Rapids, Mi: Zondervan, 2009.

Kreeft, Peter. *C. S. Lewis for the Third Millennium: Six Essays on* The Abolition of Man. San Francisco, Ca: Ignatius Press, 1994.

_____. *Fundamentals of the Faith: Essays in Christian Apologetics*. San Francisco, Ca: Ignatius Press, 1988.

_____. *Heaven: The Heart's Deepest Longing*. San Francisco, Ca: Ignatius Press, 1989.

Kreeft, Peter, and Ronald Tacelli. *Handbook of Christian Apologetics*. Downers Grove, Il: InterVarsity, 1994.

Lewis, C. S. *The Abolition of Man or Reflections on Education with Special Reference to the Teaching of English in the Upper Forms of Schools*. New York, NY: MacMillan, 1947; rpt. New York, NY: HarperOne, 1971.

_____. "Bluspels and Flalansferes: A Semantic Nightmare," *Selected Literary Essays*. Ed. Walter Hooper. Cambridge: Cambridge University Press, 1969: 251–65.

_____. "Christian Apologetics." 1945. *God in the Dock*, ed. Walter Hooper. Grand Rapids, Mi: Eerdmans, 1970: 89–103.

_____. *The Collected Letters of C. S. Lewis*, 3 vols., ed. Walter Hooper. San Francisco, Ca: HarperSanFrancisco, 2004.

_____. *The Collected Poems of C. S. Lewis*, ed. Don W. King. Kent, Oh: Kent State University Press, 2015.

_____. "Cross Examination." Orig. printed as "I Was Decided Upon," *Decision* II (Sept. 1963): 3 and "Heaven, Earth, and Outer Space," *Decision* II (Oct. 1963): 4; rpt. *God in the Dock: Essays on Theology and Ethics*. Ed. Walter Hooper. Grand Rapids, Mi: Eerdmans, 1970: 258–67.

_____. "God in the Dock." As "Difficulties in Presenting the Faith to Modern Unbelievers," *Lumen Vitae* III (Sept. 1948): 421–6; rpt.

God in the Dock: Essays on Theology and Ethics. Ed. Walter Hooper. Grand Rapids, Mi: Eerdmans, 1970: 240–44.

_____. *God in the Dock: Essays on Theology and Ethics.* Ed. Walter Hooper. Grand Rapids, Mi: Eerdmans, 1970.

_____. *The Great Divorce.* New York, NY: MacMillan, 1946.

_____. "Is Theology Poetry?" Paper read to the Oxford Socratic Club, 6 November 1944. *The Socratic Digest* 3 (1945); rpt. *The Weight of Glory and Other Addresses.* Ed. Walter Hooper. San Francisco, Ca: HarperCollins, 1980: 116–140.

_____. *The Last Battle.* 1955; New York, NY: HarperCollins, 1984.

_____. "Learning in Wartime." Sermon preached at St. Mary the Virgin, Oxford, 22 Oct. 1939. *The Weight of Glory and Other Addresses.* Ed. Walter Hooper. San Francisco, Ca: HarperCollins, 1980: 47–63.

_____. *The Lion, the Witch, and the Wardrobe.* 1950; New York, NY: HarperCollins, 1978.

_____. "Man or Rabbit?" S.C.M., 1946; rpt. *God in the Dock: Essays on Theology and Ethics.* Ed. Walter Hooper. Grand Rapids, Mi: Eerdmans, 1970: 108–113.

_____. "Meditation in a Toolshed." *God in the Dock: Essays on Theology and Ethics.* Ed. Walter Hooper. Grand Rapids, Mi: Eerdmans, 1970: 212–15.

_____. *Mere Christianity.* New York, NY: MacMillan, 1943.

_____. *Miracles: A Preliminary Study.* New York, NY: MacMillan, 1947.

_____. "Modern Theology and Biblical Criticism," *Christian Reflections.* Ed. Walter Hooper. Grand Rapids, Mi: Eerdmans, 1967: 152–66.

_____. "Myth Become Fact," *God in the Dock: Essays on Theology and Ethics,* ed. Walter Hooper. Grand Rapids, Mi: Eerdmans, 1970: 63–67.

_____. "On Obstinacy in Belief." *The Sewanee Review*, Autumn, 1955; rpt. *The World's Last Night and other Essays*. New York, NY: Harcourt, Brace & World, 1960: 13–30.

_____. *Out of the Silent Planet*. 1938; New York, NY: Simon & Schuster Inc., 1996.

_____. *Perelandra*. 1943; New York, NY: Scribner, 1996.

_____. *The Pilgrim's Regress: an Allegorical Apology for Christianity, Reason, and Romanticism*. 1933; Grand Rapids, Mi: Eerdmans, 1960.

_____. *Poems*, ed. Walter Hooper. New York, NY: Harcourt Brace Jovanovich, 1964.

_____. *Prince Caspian*. 1951; New York, NY: HarperCollins, 1979.

_____. *The Problem of Pain*. 1940; New York, NY: MacMillan, 1967.

_____. "Rejoinder to Dr. Pittenger." *The Christian Century* LXXV (26 Nov. 1958): 1359–61; rpt. *God in the Dock*, ed. Walter Hooper. Grand Rapids, Mi: Eerdmans, 1970: 177–83.

_____. "Religion: Reality or Substitute?" *World Dominion* XIX (Sept.-Oct. 1941); rpt. *Christian Reflections*, ed. Walter Hooper. Grand Rapids, Mi: Eerdmans, 1967: 37–43.

_____. *The Silver Chair*. 1953; New York, NY: HarperCollins, 1979.

_____. "Sometimes Fairy Stories May Say Best What's to be Said." *Of Other World: Essays and Stories*. Ed. Waler Hooper. New York, NY: Harcourt Brace Jovanovich, 1966.

_____. *Surprised by Joy: The Shape of my Early Life*. New York, NY: Harcourt, Brace, and World, 1955.

_____. *Till We Have Faces: A Myth Retold*. Harcourt Brace & World, 1956; rpt. Grand Rapids, Mi: Eerdmans, 1968.

_____. "Transposition." Sermon preached in the chapel of St.

Mansfield College, Oxford, 28 May 1944. *The Weight of Glory and Other Addresses*. Ed. Walter Hooper. San Francisco, Ca: HarperCollins, 1980: 91–115.

_____. *The Voyage of the Dawn Treader*. 1952; New York, NY: HarperCollins, 1980.

Markos, Louis. *Lewis Agonistes: How C. S. Lewis can Train us to Wrestle with the Modern and Postmodern World*. Nashville, Tn: Broadman, 2003.

McGrath, Alister. *C. S. Lewis: A Life*. Carol Stream, Il: Tyndale, 2013.

McGrew, Lydia. *Hidden in Plain View: Undesigned Coincidences in the Gospels and Acts*. Chillicothe, Oh: DeWard, 2017.

_____. *The Mirror or the Mask: Liberating the Gospels from Literary Devices*. Tampa, Fl: DeWard, 2019.

Mills, David, ed. *The Pilgrim's Guide: C. S. Lewis and the Art of Witness*. Grand Rapids, Mi: Eerdmans, 1998.

Mitchell, Christopher W. "Bearing the Weight of Glory: The Cost of C.S. Lewis's Witness." In David Mills, ed., *The Pilgrim's Guide: C. S. Lewis and the Art of Witness*. Grand Rapids, Mi: Eerdmans, 1998: 3–14.

Menuge, Angus J. L., ed., *C. S. Lewis, Lightbearer in the Shadowlands: The Evangelistic Vision of C. S. Lewis*. Wheaton, Il: Crossway, 1997.

Montgomery, John Warwick, ed. *Myth, Allegory, and Gospel: An Interpretation of J. R. R. Tolkien, C. S. Lewis, G. K. Chesterton, and Charles Williams*. Minneapolis, Mn: Bethany Press, 1974.

_____. *Tractatus Logico-Theologicus*. Bonn: Verlag fur Kultur and Wissenschaft, 2005.

Moore, Dwayne. "The Argument from Reason and the Dual Process Reply." *Philosophia Christi* 24:2 (2022): 217-39.

Moreland, J. P. *The God Question: An Invitation to a Life of Meaning*. Eugene, Or: Harvest House, 2009.

_____. *Scaling the Secular City: A Defense of Christianity*. Grand Rapids, Mi: Baker, 1987.

Morison, Frank. *Who Moved the Stone?* Downers Grove, Il: Inter Varsity Press, n.d.

Neill, Stephen. *The Interpretation of the New Testament, 1861–1961*. New York, NY: Oxford University Press, 1966.

Nicholi, Armand M., Jr. *The Question of God: C. S. Lewis and Sigmund Freud Debate God, Love, Sex, and the Meaning of Life*. New York, NY: Free Press, 2002.

O'Hara, David L. "Con: C.S. Lewis on Evil: At Best a Likely Story." *C. S. Lewis's Apologetics: Pro and Con*. Ed. Gregory Bassham. Leiden: Brill/Rodopi, 2015: 227–36.

Poe, Harry Lee. *Becoming C. S. Lewis: A Biography of Young Jack Lewis (1898–1918)*. Wheaton, Il: Crossway, 2019.

_____. *The Completion of C. S. Lewis: From War to Joy (1948–1963)*. Wheaton, Il: Crossway, 2022.

_____. *The Making of C. S. Lewis: From Atheist to Apologist (1918–1943)*. Wheaton, Il: Crossway, 2021.

Polanyi, Michael. *Personal Knowledge: Towards a Post-Critical Philosophy*. New York, NY: Harper & Row, 1964.

Purtill, Richard L *C. S. Lewis's Case for the Christian Faith*. San Francisco, Ca: Harper and Row, 1981.

Reppert, Victor. *C. S. Lewis's Dangerous Idea: In Defense of the Argument from Reason*. Downers Grove, Il: InterVarsity Pr., 2003.

_____. "The Lewis-Anscombe Controversy: A Discussion of the Issues." *Christian Scholar's Review* 19:1 (Sept., 1989): 32–48.

_____. "Pro: The Argument from Reason Defended." Bassham, Gregory, ed. *C. S. Lewis's Apologetics: Pro and Con*. Leiden: Brill/Rodopi, 2015: 75–89.

_____. "Reply to David Kyle Johnson." *C. S. Lewis's Apologetics: Pro and Con.* Ed. Gregory Bassham. Leiden: Brill/Rodopi, 2015: 105–111.

Richardson, Cyril C., ed. *Early Christian Fathers.* Vol. 1 of *The Library of Christian Classics,* ed. John Baillie, John T. McNeill, and Henry P. Van Dusen. Philadelphia, Pa: Westminster, 1953.

Rickakabaugh, Brandon, and Todd Buras. "The Argument from Reason and Mental Causal Drainage." *Philosophia Christi* 19:2 (2017): 381–99.

Rigney, Joe. *Lewis and the Christian Life: Becoming fully Human in the Presence of God.* Wheaton, Il: Crossway, 2018.

Root, Jerry and Mark Neal. *The Surprising Imagination of C. S. Lewis: An Introduction.* Nashville, Tn: Abingdon, 2015.

Sayer, George. *Jack: A Life of C. S. Lewis.* Wheaton, Il: Crossway, 1994.

Schaeffer, Francis. *The God Who is There: Speaking Historic Christianity into the Twentieth Century.* Downers Grove, Il: Inter-Varsity Press, 1958.

_____. *The Mark of the Christian.* Downers Grove, Il: Inter-Varsity Press, 1970.

Schultz, Jefferey D. & John G. West, Jr., eds. *The C. S. Lewis Reader's Encyclopedia.* Grand Rapids, Mi: Zondervan, 1998.

Starr, Charlie W. *The Faun's Bookshelf: C. S. Lewis on Why Myth Matters.* Kent, Oh: Black Squirrel Books, 2018.

Strobel, Lee. *The Case for a Creator.* Grand Rapids, Mi: Zondervan, 2004.

_____. *The Case for Christ: A Journalist's Personal Investigation of the Evidence for Jesus.* Grand Rapids, Mi: Zondervan, 1998.

Tallon, Philip. "Pro: *The Problem of Pain* Defended." *C. S. Lewis's Christian Apologetics: Pro .and Con.* Ed/ Gregory Bassham. Leiden" Brill/Rodopi, 2015: 211–225.

Tixier, Eliane, "Imagination Baptized," *The Longing for a Form: Essays on the Fiction of C. S. Lewis,* ed. Peter J. Schackel (Grand Rapids, Mi: Baker, 1971): 136–58.

Tolkien, J. R. R. "On Fairie Stories." *The Tolkien Reader*. New York, NY: Ballantine, 1966: 3–73.

Traherne, Thomas. "Centuries of Meditation." *Seventeenth-Century Prose and Poetry*, 2nd ed., ed. Alexander M Witherspoon. and Frank J. Warnke. New York, NY: Harcourt Brace Jovanovich, 1982, 694–704.

Vaus, Will. *Mere Theology: A Guide to the Thought of C. S. Lewis*. Downers Grove, Il: InterVarsity Press, 2004.

Veith, Jr., Gene Edward. "A Vision, Within a Dream, Within the Truth: C. S. Lewis as Evangelist to the Postmodernists." In Menuge, Angus J. L., ed., *C. S. Lewis, Lightbearer in the Shadowlands: The Evangelistic Vision of C. S. Lewis*. Wheaton, Il: Crossway, 1997: 367–87.

Walsh, Chad. *C. S. Lewis: Apostle to the Skeptics*. New York, NY: Mac-Millan, 1949.

―――――. *The Literary Legacy of C. S. Lewis*. New York, NY: Harcourt Brace Jovanovich, 1979.

Ward, Michael. *After Humanity: A Guide to C. S. Lewis's* The Abolition of Msn. `Park Ridge, Il: Word on Fire Academic, 2021.

Wielenberg, Erik J. "Con: A Critique of the Moral Argument. *C. S. Lewis's Christian Apologetics: Pro and Con*. Ed. Gregory Bassham. Leiden: Rodopi, 2015: 141–151.

―――――. *God and the Reach of Reason*. New York, NY: Cambridge University Press, 2008.

Williams, Donald T. "Anselm and Aslan: C. S. Lewis and The Ontological Argument." *Touchstone: A Journal of Mere Christianity* 27:6 (Nov.-Dec. 2014): 36–39.

―――――. "Answers for Orual: C. S. Lewis as a role Model for Winsome Apologists," (2016 Presidential Address from the annual meeting of the International Society for Christian Apologetics), *The Journal of the International Society of Christian Apologetics* 10:1 (March, 2017): 5–20.

―――――. "An Apologist's Evening Prayer: Reflecting on C. S. Lewis's Reflections on the Psalms." In Edwards, Bruce L., Jr., ed. *C. S. Lewis: Life, Works, Legacy*, 4 vols. London: Praeger, 2007, 3:237–56.

_____. "The Argument from Desire Revisited." *The Lamp-Post of the Southern California C. S. Lewis Society* 32:1 (Spring 2010): 32–33.

_____. "C.S. Lewis: Defender of the Faith," *Christian Research Journal* 40:2 (April, 2017): 10–17.

_____. "Cartographer of the Divine: C.S. Lewis as *Doctor Ecclesiae*," *Inklings Forever* IX (2014).

_____. "A Closer Look at the 'Unorthodox' Lewis." *Christianity Today* (Dec. 21, 1979): 24–27.

_____. *Deeper Magic: The Theology behind the Writings of C. S, Lewis*. Baltimore, Md: Square Halo Books, 2016.

_____. *An Encouraging Thought: The Christian Worldview in the Writings of J. R. R. Tolkien*. Cambridge, Oh: Christian Publishing House, 2018.

_____. "'For the Sake of the Story': Doctrine and Discernment in Reading C.S. Lewis," *Modern Reformation* 18:3 (May-June, 2009): 33–36.

_____. "G. K. Chesterton, *The Everlasting Man*." *C. S. Lewis's List: The Ten Books that Influenced Him Most*. Ed. David Werther and Susan Werther. New York, NY: Bloomsbury, 2015: 31–48.

_____. "Identity Check: Are C.S. Lewis's Critics Right, or Is His 'Trilemma' Valid?" *Touchstone: a Journal of Mere Christianity* 23:3 (May-June 2010): 25–29.

_____. *Inklings of Reality: Essays toward a Christian Philosophy of Letters*. Toccoa Falls, Ga: Toccoa Falls College Press, 1996; 2nd ed., revised and expanded, Lynchburg, Va: Lantern Hollow Press, 2012.

_____. "'Is Man a Myth?': Mere Christian Perspectives on the Human," *Mythlore* 23:1 (Summer/fall 2000): 4–19.

_____. "Lacking, Ludicrous, or Logical? The Validity of Lewis's 'Trilemma.'" *Midwestern Journal of Theology* 11:1 (Spring 2012): 91–102.

_____. "Lions of Succession: On Being a Free Narnian & the Joy of Subordination'" *Touchstone: A Journal of Mere Christianity* 18:3 (April 2005): 15–17.

_____. "Literature for Wisdom: Donald T. Williams on Reading in the Service of Christian Living," *Touchstone: A Journal of Mere Christianity* 33:4 (July/August 2020): 20–22.

_____. "Made for Another World: C.S. Lewis's Argument from Desire Revisited." *Philosophia Christi: The Journal of the Evangelical Philosophical Society* 19:2 (2018): 449–54.

_____. "Meaningful Truth: The Critical Role of Imagination in the Work of C.S. Lewis," *Touchstone: A Journal of Mere Christianity* 31:6 (Nov.-Dec., 2018): 34–37.

_____. *Mere Humanity: G.K. Chesterton, C. S. Lewis, and J.R.R. Tolkien on the Human Condition.* Nashville, Tn: Broadman, 2006.

_____. *Ninety-Five Theses for a New Reformation: A Road Map for Post-Evangelical Christianity.* Toccoa, Ga: *Semper Reformanda* Publications, 2021.

_____. *The Person and Work of the Holy Spirit.* Nashville, Tn: Broadman & Holman, 1994; reprint Eugene, Or: Wipf and Stock.

_____. "Printing Error: On Anscombe's Final Word on Lewis and Naturalism." *Touchstone: A Journal of Mere Christianity* 29:3 (May-June 2016): 20–22.

_____. "Pro: A Defense of C.S. Lewis's 'Trilemma.'" *C. S. Lewis's Apologetics: Pro and Con.* Ed. Gregory Bassham. Leiden: Brill/Rodopi, 2015: 171–89. (Note: There is a typo in the book. The chapter is by Donald T. Williams. Donald S. Williams does not exist.)

_____. *Reflections from Plato's Cave: Essays in Evangelical Philosophy.* Lynchburg, Va: Lantern Hollow Press, 2012.

_____. "Reply to Adam Barkman," *C. S. Lewis's Apologetics: Pro and Con,* ed. Gregory Bassham (Leiden: Brill/Rodopi, 2015): 201–4.

_____. Review of *C. S. Lewis and the Search for Rational Religion*, 2nd ed., by John Beversluis, *Mythlore: The Journal of the Mythopoeic Society* 105/106, Spring/Summer 2009): 168–70.

_____. Review of *C. S. Lewis's Dangerous Idea*, by Victor Reppert (Downers Grove, Il: IVP, 2003), *Philosophia Christi*, 6:2 (2004): 375–77.

_____. Review of *Lewis Agonistes: How C. S. Lewis Can Train us to Wrestle with the Modern and Postmodern World*, by Louis Markos (Nashville, Tn: Broadman, 2003), *Mythprint* 43:9 (September 2006): 11–12.

_____. Review of *The Pilgrim's Guide: C. S. Lewis and the Art of Witness*, ed. David Mills (Grand Rapids, Mi: Eerdmans, 1998), in *The Lamp-post* 23:2 (Summer 1999): 36–37.

_____. "Text vs. Word: C.S. Lewis's Doctrine of Inspiration and the Inerrancy of Scripture," *I Am Put Here for the Defense of the Gospel: A Festschrift for Nom Geisler*, ed. terry L. Miethe (Eugene, Or: Wipf and Stock, 2016): 153–69.

_____. *The Young Christian's Survival Guide: Common Questions Young Christians are Asked about God, the Bible, and the Christian Faith Answered*. Cambridge, Oh: Christian Publishing House, 2019.

Williams, Peter S. "Pro: A Defense of C.S. Lewis's Argument from Desire." *C. S. Lewis's Christian Apologetics: Pro and Con*. Ed. Gregory Bassham. Leiden: Rodopi, 2015: 27–44.

_____. "Reply to Gregory Bassham." *C. S. Lewis's Christian Apologetics: Pro and Con*. Ed. Gregory Bassham. Leiden: Rodopi, 2015: 57–68.

Wright, N. T. "Simply Lewis: Reflections on a Master Apologist after 60 Years." *Touchstone: A Journal of Mere Christianity* 20:2 (March, 2007): 28–33.

Young, Frances. "A Cloud of Witnesses." *The Myth of God Incarnate*. Ed. John Hick. Philadelphia, Pa: Westminster, 1977: 13–47.

INDEX